WHITE PEARL
Names and Descriptions of the Single Monad

by the Greatest Master
Muhyiddin Ibn al-Arabi

translation and annotation by
Mohamed Haj Yousef

PAPERBACK: ISBN: 978-1093229295

All rights reserved. No part of this book may be reprinted or reproduced or utilized in any form or by any electronic, mechanical, or other means, now known or hereafter invented, including photocopying and recording, or in any information storage or retrieval system, without permission in writing from the author.
Copyright Mohamed Haj Yousef
UNITED ARAB EMIRATES UNIVERSITY
First Release: July 2019

This book is a translation of Ibn al-Arabi's short treatise called: *al-Durrah al-Bayddaa*, in which Ibn al-Arabi answers a question about the Single Monad, or the Universal Intellect, thus elaborating on its nature and enumerating some of its names and descriptions. In the Single Monad Model, we quoted many paragraphs from this book, so here we give a full translation with extensive commenting and explanation.

This is the third book in the Short Treatises By Ibn al-Arabi book series.
The first book in this series is: That Is All Indeed: what the Seeker Needs (ISBN: 9781482077421).
The second book is: Eternity: ab ante - a post (ISBN: 9781798666555), published June 2019.
More information: http://www.ibnalarabi.com

Dedication:

- to the Greatest Master Muhyiddin Ibn al-Arabi and all his students and admirers.

Contents

Dedication iii
Preface vii

Introduction (by Mohamed Haj Yousef) 1

About Muhyiddin Ibn al-Arabi 1
About this Book: 8
Printed Editions: 13
Available Manuscripts: 14
The Different Names of the Single Monad: 21
The Oneness of Being: 27
The Single-Monad Model: 31
The Duality of Time Theory: 34
What is the Single Monad: 37
The Structure of the Monad: 39
The Greatest Element: 41
The White Pearl in the Other Books 43

The White Pearl (by Ibn al-Arabi) 49

[Introduction:] 49
[The Self-Existence of Allah:] 49
[Potential Existence:] 50
[The Becoming of the World:] 52
[The Re-creation of the World:] 55
[The Single Monad:] 57
[Some of the Various Names of the Single Monad:] . . 58

[The Eternal Existence of Allah:] 69
[The Temporal Existence of the Intellect:] 69
[The Perpetual Emanation:] 70
[Divine Generosity:] 70
[Endurance and Permanence:] 71
[His Perfection:] 73
[His Completeness:] 73
[So He is Created:] 74
[The Length and Breadth of Spirits and Bodies:] 74
[His Length and Breadth are Equal:] 75
[The Origin of the Sexagesimal System:] 76
[The Cyclic Nature of Existence:] 77
[The Emanation of the Intellect:] 81
[The Choice of Creation:] 82
[The Multiple Descriptions of the Intellect:] 82
[The Choice of Allah, the Exalted:] 83
[The One-to-Many Relation:] 84
[The Types of Descriptions:] 93
[How Multiplicity is Emerging:] 95
[The Effect of Ability:] 96
[The Concurrence of Causes and Results:] 98
[The Apparent Order of the World:] 100
[Conclusion:] 101

Books by Mohamed Haj Yousef 103

References and Bibliography 111

The Original Arabic Text 111

Preface

About this Book

This book is a translation of Ibn al-Arabi's short treatise: *"al-Durrah al-Bayddaa"* ("the White Pearl"), a designation that refers to the Universal Intellect, that is also called: "the Single Monad". In the Single Monad book series, we quoted many paragraphs from this book, so here we present a full translation with some comments and explanations.

In this book, the author illuminates some of the various names and descriptions of the Single Monad and how multiplicity is emerging, or emanating, from absolute Oneness. As we explained in the previous books, *time* is the link that explains this one-to-many relation, which is normally referred to as the Oneness of Being.

Therefore, understanding the real flow of time, and its apparent dualistic nature represented by the genuinely-complex time-time geometry, is necessary to understand the ultimate Oneness of Being, and thus reveal the connection between the various apparent dualities manifested on many fundamental levels in nature, such as discreteness and continuity, particles and waves, energy and matter, time and space, and more generally: physics and mathematics.

Understanding these concepts is quite essential in solving the major problems in physics and cosmology, including those arising from singularities and infinities. In fact, because in the Single Monad Model the whole world is dynamically formed from only one monad, the White Pearl, as a designation given to this Single Monad, is equivalent to the modern view of conceiving the cosmos as a "white hole", since we are living inside it, as opposed to the "black hole" that forms a singularity in our space-time.

Moreover, as we shall see further below, this book is often found in a series that include also "the Black Bead", whose descriptions correspond to the modern concept of the black hole. What is even more interesting is that these "jewels" exist also in other colors, such as the "Green Emerald" and "Red Ruby". However, as we shall see in this book, these objects have both material and abstract dimensions, ans that's why they have so many names, that correspond to some aspects of their physical and spiritual behavior, and other descriptions.

In chapter 47 of the Meccan Revelations, to explain this one-to-many relation, Ibn al-Arabi employs the example of a **circle**, whose central point is the *indivisible* Single Monad that meets *at the same time* all the multiplicity of creation represented by the circumference. This paradoxical relation, between the Creator and the creations, is in clear apparent contradiction with the widely accepted philosophical maxim — a central assumption in the prevailing contemporary philosophical cosmology of Ibn Sina and his followers — that "from the One only one may emerge (or proceed)" (*la yasdur an al-waahid illa waahid*).

Logically, when speaking about physical objects and dimensions, it is not possible to imagine a relation between the One and the many without affecting the unique Oneness (ahadiyya) of the One. In mathematics and geometry, this example of the circle works only due to the infinitely small (or dimensionless) points, while the contemporary science of physics and cosmology deals with corporeal worlds that have dimensions. Therefore, Ibn al-Arabi's unique understanding of time shall provide the essential link between physics and mathematics, or between reality and imagination, in the same way as it does provide the necessary link between Oneness and multiplicity.

Ibn al-Arabi quotes this emanationist philosophical maxim quite often [I.42.14, I.260.5, II.31.14]. However, although he disagrees with this general proposition [I.260.5, I.715.12, II.434.20], he sometimes explains further that this notion can be held true for physical beings but not for Allah Himself, because He is the Creator, and He is the unique One, Who can obviously create multiple creations as we can clearly see in the surrounding world.

In order to understand the relation between the unique Oneness of the Real and the multiplicity of the creatures, Ibn al-Arabi adds time to the previous philosophical statement, which can be then reformulated as: "from the

One only one can proceed at a time". This re-statement is indeed the key to understanding his unique views of time and the Oneness of Being. In this way the world is created by Allah "in series", and not just as one single act. However, in this book of the White Pearl, the author affirms that this particular mode of creation was chosen by Allah to be like that, although in fact He might have done it in any other way, so it is not an (external) restriction imposed over Him.

We also showed, in the first volume of the Single Monad Model, that the meaning of this principle (or re-creation, or creation is series) is in fact derived directly from the well-known verse in the Quran: (each Day He is upon some (one, single) task) [55:29]. Ibn al-Arabi quotes this verse most frequently in his discussion on time, and this explains the basis of his ultimate quantization of the space-time geometry itself, without any prior background.

Note About Transliteration

In this book, we use a transliteration style that avoids using any unusual characters. This simplified system is straightforward, so we don't need to add any table of definitions. For example: a double "aa" indicates *alif-madda*, while a double "ee" or "ii" is *yaa-madda*. Other Arabic sounds that do not have English equivalents will be transliterated to the nearest familiar sound, sometimes also using double letters, such as "dd", "ss" and "tt" (for: "ddad", "ssad" and"ttaa", respectively).

Although this system might cause some confusion, but it should be not very difficult for professionals seeking further information to distinguish the correct pronunciation of these transliterated Arabic words or letters. However, this simplified transliteration is more compatible with e-book readers and online publishing and encoding.

Note About References and Bibliography

In addition to the usual bibliographical references that will be included at the end of this book, and referenced properly in the text, most of the other quotes are based on Ibn al-Arabi's major comprehensive work of the "Meccan Revelations" ("Al-Futuhat Al-Makkiyya"), or: Futuhat, for short.

Therefore, because we are going to refer to this book very often, we shall use a short reference style directly in the text, without using footnotes, enclosed by medium brackets in the form: [*Futuhat*: X.000.00], which means: [*Futuhat*: volume.page.line]. When the line number is omitted, the reference is to be found in the entire page, or a range of pages like this [*Futuhat*: II.229-231]. For all this, we have used the standard edition re-published by many houses based on (photocopy of) the old edition of Bulaq, published in 1911, in four volumes each about 600-700 pages of 35 lines, as it will be also listed in the Bibliography. It should be noticed, however, that newer type-scripted editions may be different although some of them are also four volumes.

All references to the Holy Quran shall be indicated also inside the text; after each verse quoted or meaning indicated, we shall add a reference like that [*Quran*: xx.yy] where xx refers to the number of Sura (chapter) and yy is the number of Aya (verse).

References to Hadith, narrations after the Prophet Muhammad peace be upon him, are mostly quoted from the Hadith collection: Kanz al-Ummal, collected by Ali ibn Abd-al-Malik al-Hindi (1472 CE / 888 AH - 1567 CE / 975 AH). It was first Published by Daairat al-Maarif, Hyderabad Deccan, and now available from other publishers, such as Dar al-Kutub al-Ilmiyyah, Lebanon, published in 1998, edited by Mahmud Umar al-Dumyati. References from this collections are given in the form [*Kanz*: Hadtih number].

IBNALARABI.COM Website

For more information about the Greatest Master Muhyiddin Ibn al-Arabi and his heritage, please check:
http://www.ibnalarabi.com.

This website contains many manuscripts, books and articles, in Arabic, English, and other languages, about Ibn al-Arabi and related studies, in addition to the discussion forums.

We would like also to invite all interested readers and visitors to participate in enriching this website with their opinions and essays by participating in the forums or adding comments on the various articles, or even publishing their own articles in the various sections of the site.

The contents of this website vary from one language to another; but most of it is in Arabic and English, and some articles are translated into or from other languages.

This website is supervised by Mohamed Haj Yousef, and most of the information about Ibn al-Arabi is derived from the book: the Sun from the West (in Arabic), that will be available in English by the end of 2019, God willing!

Author:

> Mohamed bin Ali Haj Yousef
> Friday, June 28, 2019
> United Arab Emirates University
> Al-Ain, United Arab Emirates

Introduction
(by Mohamed Haj Yousef)

"The Real has a unique aspect towards everything, ... and every (single) thing is one, ... and He is One. So only one is proceeding from Him (at a time), and He is always in the oneness of every one."

Ibn al-Arabi, *The Meccan Revelations, II.434.23*

About Muhyiddin Ibn al-Arabi

This brief introduction about Ibn al-Arabi is extracted from "the Sun from the West" (Yousef, 2019) which is a translation of Shams-ul-Maghrib published in Arabic (Yousef, 2006), (Yousef, 2013):

The Greatest Master Muhyiddin Ibn al-Arabi is Muhammad bin Ali bin Muhammad bin Ahmed bin Abdullah al-Hatimi al-Taei, descendant of Abdallah ibn Hatim, brother of Udei bin Hatim, the companion of the Prophet Muhammad, peace be upon him. He is known as Abu Abdullah, al-Hatimi, al-Taei, Ibn Arab, or Ibn al-Arabi, and he is often designated as the Greatest Sheikh (Doctor Maximus), Muhyiddin (Reviver of Religion), Imam of the Pious, and other titles of veneration and honor he deserves.

Ibn al-Arabi was born on the night of Monday, the 17th of Ramadan 560 AH, that is the 26th of July 1165 AD, in the city of Murcia in eastern Andalusia. He then moved with his family to Seville in the year 568/1172, where he lived for the next twenty years, during which he traveled to Morocco and Tunisia several times, and stayed there for intermittent periods, before traveling to the East for the purpose of Hajj in the year 598/1201, never to return back to Andalusia. In the East he stayed in Egypt briefly and then went through Palestine, heading to Mecca, where he devoted himself to worshiping and teaching at the Grand Sacred Mosque, the place where received the secrets and wisdom he deposited in his famous book of the Meccan Revelations. Then he went to Iraq and entered Baghdad and Mosul and met their famous Sheikhs, before traveling north to Anatolia and Turkey, where he dwelt for many years and had a high status with king Kikaws.

After that, Ibn al-Arabi took numerous trips between Iraq, Egypt, Syria and Palestine, until he finally settled in Damascus in the year 620/1223 and he stayed there until he passed away, in the night of the 22nd of the month of Rabii the Second in 638 AH corresponding to the 9th of November 1240 AD. He was buried at the foothill of Mount Kassioun, now the region where his mausoleum lies is called after his name (Sheikh Muhyiddin) where his grave is located beside the mosque which was built by Sultan Selim when he entered Damascus in 922/1516. Ibn al-Arabi, may Allah have mercy on him, had two sons: Saad Eddin and Imad Eddin.

He studied Quran in Seville on Sheikh Abu Bakr bin Khalaf al-Kawmi, according to the seven readings, using the book of al-Kafi, and he studied interpretation and heard from a number of authors or those who narrate after them, including Abu Bakr Muhammad ibn Abi Jamra, after his father who narrates directly from al-Dani, the author of al-Tayseer. He also studied under Ibn Zarkoun and Abu Muhammad Abd-ul-Haq al-Ishbili al-Azdi and many others. He also heard the hadith from Abu-l-qasim Al-Khozstani and others, and he heard Sahih Muslim from Sheikh Abu al-Hasan ibn Abi Nasr, as we summarized with more details in the introduction of the Sun from the West, from which this brief introduction is extracted.

The Greatest Sheikh Muhyiddin Ibn al-Arabi excelled in mysticism and Sufi science, in which he wrote hundreds of books and treatises, in excess of five hundred books according to Abdul Rahman Jami, author of the book "Nafahat al-Uns". One of these books is the "Meccan Revelations" considered by many as the key encyclopedic source in Islamic mysticism, and one of the most important books in the history of mankind. He also wrote a book on "the interpretation of the Quran" on which the author of Fawat al-Wafiyyat says that it spans ninety five volumes, and yet he worked only on the first half of Quran, to al-Kahf Chapter, right up to the verse speaking about the divine knowledge of Khidr: "And we have taught him the science of Ours" [18:65], but then he died before he could complete it.

He also wrote: "the Bezels of Wisdom" that

he says in his introduction that he saw the Prophet Muhammad, peace be upon him, in a dream, and he gave him a book and asked him to bring out to public, so he wrote it as it is without any addition nor dropping!

Among his other books also we mention: "Entertaining the Righteous (Muhadarat-al-Abraar)", "Originating the Circles (Inshaa al-Dawaair)", "the Bolt of the Restless (Uqlat al-Mustawfiz)", "the Fabulous Gryphon (An-qaa Mughrib)", "the Discloser of Desires (Turjuman al-Ashwaaq)", "the Divine Policies in Reforming the Human Kingdom (al-Tadbiraat al-Ilahiyya)", "the Positions of Stars (Mawaqi al-Nujum)", and many other smaller treatises.

Osman Yahya published a comprehensive study on the history and classification of Ibn al-Arabi's books(Yahya, 1964).

Many scholars and specialists agreed that Muhyiddin Ibn al-Arabi was not an ordinary author like others, but he was distinct both in quantity and quality. He himself confirms that he does not follow the course of authors who write according to their own ideology and thought, but all what he writes is inspiration from Allah. Brockelmann described him as one of the most fertile minds who has the best imagination amongst authors.

It must be noted here that Muhyiddin Ibn al-Arabi is different from the great judge Abu Bakr Muhammad bin Abdullah Ibn al-Arabi al-Maafri al-Ishbili al-Maliki, born in Seville in the year 468 AH, who is well known in jurispedance, doctrine and hadith sciences, and who has published several books, including "Law of Interpretation" and "the Lights of Dawn" and other. Sometimes people confuse between these two scholars and quote words or books for one as belonging to the other. For this reason, the people of the East began differentiating between them by calling the Greatest Sheikh by "Ibn Arabi" (without definitive article "al"), and the Judge Abu Bakr by "Ibn al-Arabi" (with the definitive article "al"). This, however, is not suitable and it did not persist, especially because the Grand Sheikh, since his birth, as well as some of his uncles and grandfathers are called by "Ibn al-Arabi", and so he signs his books, as also his early disciples used to call him. Generally now, however, we find his name either as Ibn al-Arabi or as Ibn Arabi, with and without the definitive article, but it is very easy to differentiate between these two world scholars since the first is normally known as the Grand Sheikh, Muhyiddin or Abu Abdullah, and the second is the Judge Abu Bakr al-Maliki. If none of these titles is mentioned then one can distinguish between them from the context because of their specialization, since the former is a Sufi and the latter is a jurist.

In Islamic history, however, many lesser known scholars had the title Ibn al-Arabi or Ibn al-Arabi, as Ibn al-Makola mentioned in "Ikmal". For example: Zubair Ibn al-Arabi Abu Salamah al-Nimeiri al-Basri, al-Nadr Ibn al-Arabi, Ibrahim Ibn Arab al-Kufi, Jacob Ibn al-Arabi al-Kufi, Yahya Ibn Habib Ibn al-Arabi al-Busri, Abdullah bin Muhammad bin Said bin Arabi al-Taifi, Hussein Ibn al-Arabi al-Busri, and Muhammad bin Yousef bin Arabi al-Busri.

It seems that Ahmed bin Abdullah al-Hatimi, who is the grandfather of the father of Sheikh Muhyiddin, was called the "al-Arabi", so his son, Muhammad was called "Ibn al-Arabi," and amongst the sons of Muhammad is Ali, the father of Sheikh Muhyiddin who is also named Muhammad, on the name of his grandfather, so he is: Muhammad bin Ali bin Muhammad bin Ahmed bin Abdullah al-Hatami, and he often signs his name in his books as: "Muhammad bin Ali bin Muhammad Ibn al-Arabi al-Tai al-Hatami".

In addition to this title "Muhyiddin" (the Reviver of Religion), by which he was known since his early life, his admirers often call him with venerated and revered titles such as "Sultan al-Arifin" (King of Knowers or Saints), "Imam al-Muttaqin" (the Leader of the Pious), "al-Kibrit al-Ahmar" (the Red Sulfur, meaning: Elixir), and other titles of reverence that he deserves. Starting from the tenth century AH, after Sultan Selim I entered Damascus in 922 AH, and he ordered the construction of the mosque of Sheikh Muhyiddin and building his mausoleum at his side, Ibn al-Arabi had become known as "al-Shaykh al-Akbar", the Greatest Sheikh, or Doctor Maximus.

About this Book:

The White Pearl is one of the early books written by the Greatest Sheikh Muhyiddin

Ibn al-Arabi. Although the year is exactly known, but he must have written it in the Moroccan or Andalusian period, before 598 AH / 1201 AD, because it is mentioned in his other book of Uqlat al-Mustawfiz (the Belt of the Restless) that is mentioned in the first chapters of the Meccan Revelations, that he started writing it when he settled in Mecca in that year.

We know from Ibn al-Arabi's biography, summarized in section 1 above, that he left Andalusia for the last time in 597/1200. He then stayed for short intermittent periods in the various cities in Morocco, to visit his friends of the famous Sufi masters of the time. After that he stayed in Tunisia for few months, where he stayed with his old friend Abdul-Aziz al-Mahdawi, whom he also visited in 590/1194.

Therefore, perhaps this book was written in Tunisia in response to a question from one of the followers of Sheikh Abdul-Aziz al-Mahdawi. We know that he wrote a letter to them discussing the difference between Identity and Quiddity. In Tunisia, he also started his famous book: "Establishing the Circles and Tables" (*Inshaa al-Dawaer wal-Jadawil*), but he could not complete it there because he had to resume his Hajj journey, especially that he was planning to spend the holy month of Ramadan (the ninth month of the Hijri year 598) in Egypt with early friends of childhood, Ahmed Al Khayat and Mohammed Hariri, and then pass by the blessed city of Hebron to visit the father of prophets, Prophet Ibrahim al-Khalil, peace be upon him, and then visit the Holy City of Quds, on his way to Madina, to visit the Prophet Muhammad, peace be upon him, then to reach Mecca before the start of the pilgrimage in the beginning of the month of Dhu al-Hijjah, the last month in the year 598 AH.

We also know that the introduction of the Meccan Revelations - in which he mentioned Uqlat al-Mustawfiz in which this book of al-Durrat al-Bayda was mentioned - was dedicated to Sheikh Abdul-Aziz al-Mahdawi. In this introduction, he also commented on some doctrinal issues or questions that are at the same time discussed in his other book of "the Book of Issues" (*Kitab al-Masael*), also known as the Book of (First) Knowledge. One of these issues deals with the question of the First Pen that is the Universal Intellect, the subject of this current book.

It is worth noting also that this question is often contained in a set of three issues in which the Sheikh comments of the meanings of the Intellect, the Soul, and the Body (or the Chaos: *hiyola*), which are designated as: the White pearl, the Green Emerald (and the Red Ruby), and the Black Bead, respectively. These three books are often found in one single manuscript called "the Three Questions / Issues" (*al-Masael al-Thalaath*).

It is also to be noted that these three issues may also be part of another book called "The Main Issues" (*Uyun al-Masael*), a book that is mentioned in the Index (al-Fahras) and in the Meccan Revelations.

In conclusion, it seems that the Sheikh started the Meccan Revelations with some of these fundamental doctrinal issues, which may have been extracted from the book of the Main Issues. One alternative title of this latter book is "A Foreword on how the World is Arranged" (*Khutba fi Tarteeb/Nadded al-Aalem*), but this is actually only the introduction of the Main Issues.

In the manuscript of Yusuf Agha 4868, written by Ibn al-Arabi himself as we shall mention shortly, he says: "This is the foreword of the book title as "The Means in Answering the Main Issues".

The reason why we say that the White Pearl, the Green Emerald and the Black Bead are three questions within the Main Issues is that the Sheikh mentioned at the end of the Black Bead: "We shall mention some of the things assigned to the spirits of these orbs in the part in which the answer on spirits is given, God willing". This means that there is another part of this book, that includes the answer on the Spirit, in addition to these three answers about the Intellect and the Soul and the Body, that are Pearl, the Emerald and the Bead, respectively.

It should also be noted that Sheikh Ismail Ibn Sawdekin al-Nouri has a book called "The Means of the Inquirer", in which he mentions answers to various questions he received from Sheikh Muhyiddin, whom he met in Egypt that he visited on his way from Andalusia. It seems that he asked him about these issues in the book "the Main Issues", or "The Book of Knowledge", and then he wrote the answers in this book of "The Means of the Inquirer". It seems from the analysis of many texts and manuscripts that these two books are the origin of the many titles mentioned above.[1]

Printed Editions:

The first known edition of al-Durrat al-Baydaa appeared in Cairo and Beirut in 1923, but we could not get hold of it. Then a newer version appeared in 1993, also in Cairo, by the Madbouli Library. This edition was edited by Dr. Mohamed Zainhum Mohammed Azab, who said in the introduction that he relied on some old editions (without mentioning the details, but perhaps that was the 1923 edition) and also on a manuscript found in the Egyptian Book House (Dar al-Kutub al-Massriyya, also without mentioning any more details, but perhaps he means the manuscript of Talaat 790,

---

[1] He is Abu at-Tahir, Shams al-Din Ismail Ibn Sawdekin bin Abdullah al-Nuri: a famous Sufi from Tunisia. He accompanied Sheikh Muhyiddin after he met him in Egypt, and explained some of his books. He died in 646 AH / 1248 AD.

which we will describe shortly). However, this edition contains some errors that undermine the text, although it also contains some basic sentences that are not found in the other manuscripts that we have seen, as described shortly.

More recently, this book appeared in the collection edited by Dr. Mohammed Farouk Saleh al-Badri, published in Baghdad, in 2017, by Dar Suttour.

Available Manuscripts:

To the best of our knowledge and investigation, there are no old manuscripts of this book, neither the original autograph, or nor any authenticated copies close to the seventh century AH, where the author lived. Nevertheless, there are many good manuscripts, which seem to have been copied in the last few centuries, after the end of the first millennium AH.

Among these manuscripts, there is a good copy is written in a clear modern script located in the collection Veliyuddin 1821, from page 238 to 244, which we adopted for this edition. The attached images show the beginning and end of this manuscript.

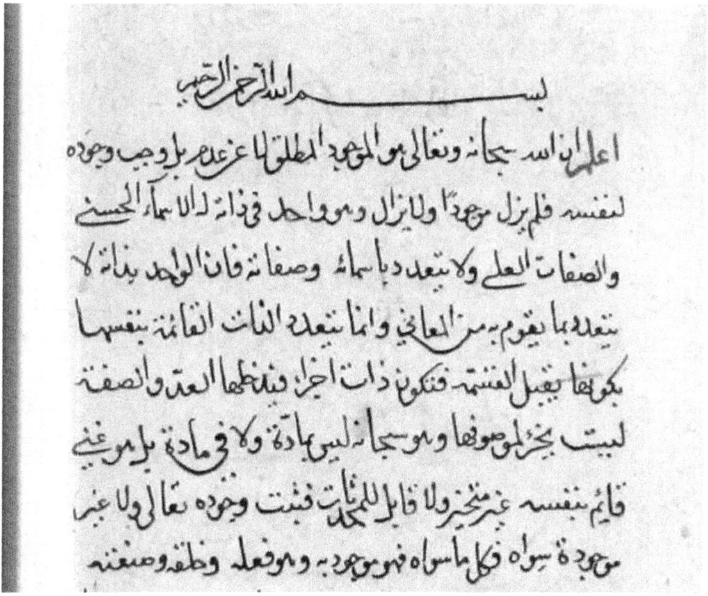

بسم الله الرحمن الرحيم
اعلم ان الله سبحانه وتعالى هو الموجود المطلق لما عز عن عدم بل وجب وجوده
لنفسه فلم يزل موجودا ولا يزال وهو واحد في ذاته له الاسماء الحسنى
والصفات العلى ولا يتعدد باسمائه وصفاته فان الواحد بذاته لا
يتعدد بما يقوم به من المعاني وانما يتعدد الذات القائمة بنفسها
بكونها يقبل القسمة فتكون ذات اجزاء فيتخللها العدم والصفة
ليست بجزء لموصوفها وهو سبحانه ليس بمادة ولا في مادة بل هو غني
قائم بنفسه غير متحيز ولا قابل للمحدثات فثبت وجوده تعالى ولا غير
موجود سواه فكل ما سواه فهو موجود به وهو فعله وخلقه وصنعته

Figure 1: The beginning of the manuscript of Veliyuddin 1821.

واجبا يتنصيته العقل لا تقتضي ايضا ان يصرالواجب ممكنا والممكن ذلك
الى بطلان الحقائق ولربق بايدينا علم الاصل فلا يدان بقى الممكن ممكنا
لا لنفسه موممكن والواجب واجبا لا لنفسه موواجب والمحال
محالا لنفسه لا محال فهذا بعض ما اجرى الله تعالى فى الوقت
على صنيعة من الجواب فى هذه المسئلة وبسطنا القول فيها فيها
وكرنا من اجل فهم الناظر فيها فان ليس كل فهم يكون له سعة التفوق
وفهم الكلام الموجز واسجما يه ينفعنا بالعلم
وجعلنا من اهله بمنه وكرمه ثم الجواب والله
الوهاب الجواد المحسن وصلى الله على سيدنا
محمد وآله وصحبه وسلم تسليما
كثيرا ابدا ابا الى يوم
الدين

Available Manuscripts: 17

We also compared the text with another good manuscript that we could not confirm its origin, but it is written in a beautiful and clear handwriting, dated in the month of Muharram in 1031 AH, and is well compatible with the previous Veliyuddin copy. We also show here the beginning and end of this manuscript.

We also compared with one manuscript found in the library of Mecca, collection number 3939. This collection also includes the three letters: the White Pearl, the Green Emerald and the Black Bead, but it is written in a compressed and unclear handwriting in some places.

There is another manuscript in Ismail Saib collection number 1197, but we could not check it. This is also the case for the manuscript in the National Library of Tunisia, bearing the number 8572 Sadikiyya, and also the manuscript of the Library of Awqaf in Baghdad, which bears the number of 7071. Another manuscript is also found in Princess Fayza collection, library of the University of Alexandria, which bears the number 154561. This collection also includes the answers of the Green Emerald and the Black Bead.

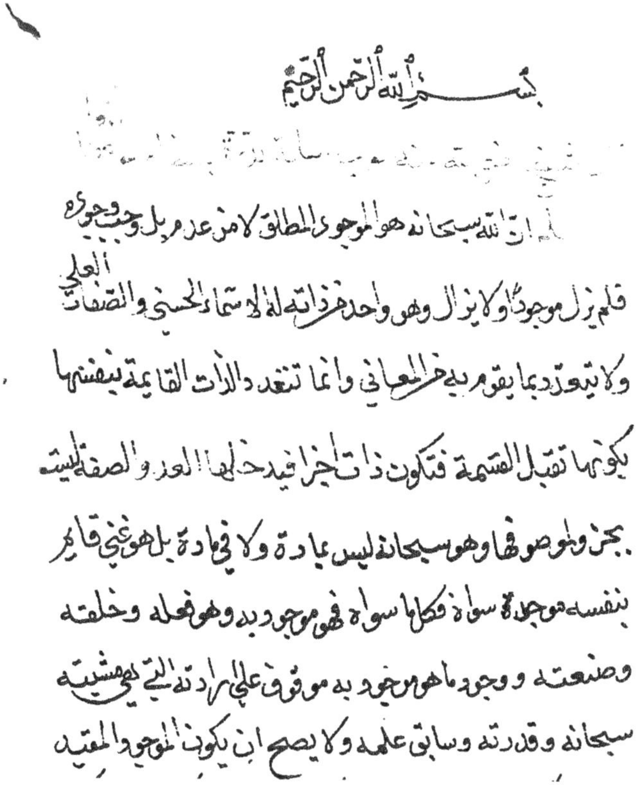

بسم الله الرحمن الرحيم

... ...

إن الله سبحانه هو الموجود المطلق لا من عدم بل وجب وجوده
فلم يزل موجوداً ولا يزال وهي واحد هذه ذاته لا اسماء الحسنى والصفات العلى
ولا يتوحّد بما يقوم بيه من المعاني وإنما تنعقد دلالات القائمة بنفسها
يكونها تقبل القسمة فتكون ذا تجزٍ فيدخلها العدم والصفة ليست
بجزء من موصوفها وهو سبحانه ليس بمادة ولا في مادة بل هو غني قائم
بنفسه موجدة سواه فكل ما سواه فهو موجود بديع وهو فعله وخلقه
وصنعته ووجود ما هو موجود به موقوف على إرادته التي هي مشيئته
سبحانه وقدرته وسابق علمه ولا يصح أن يكون الموجود المقيد

Figure 3: Beginning of the second manuscript.

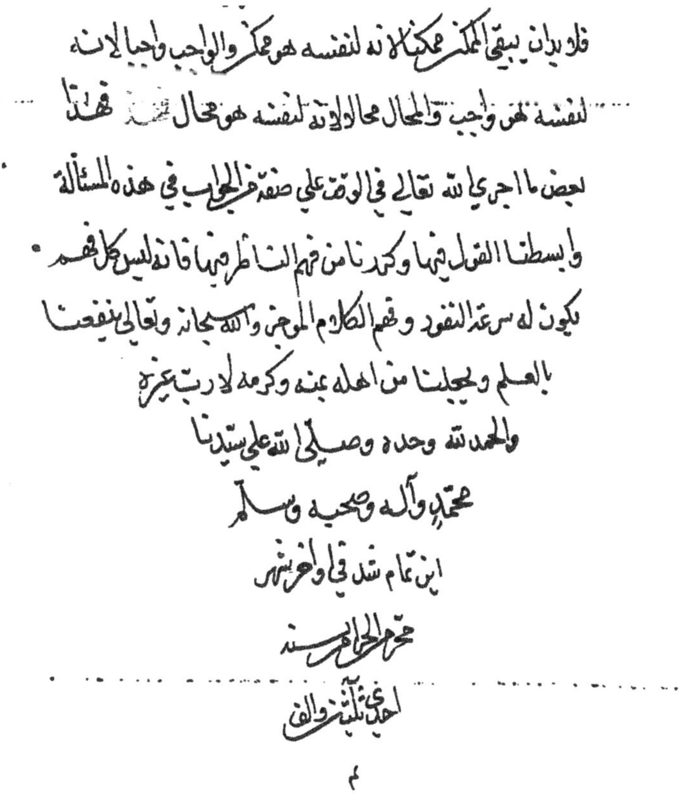

فلا بد أن يبقى الممكن ممكنًا لا أنه لنفسه هو ممكن والواجب وأجبًا لأنه
لنفسه هو واجب والمحال والمحال لا لأنه لنفسه هو محال فهذا
بعض ما أجرى الله تعالى في الوقت على صفة من الجواب في هذه المسألة
وبسطنا القول فيها وكررنا من فهم الناظر فيها فإنه ليس كل فهم
يكون له سعة للنقود وفهم الكلام الموجز والله سبحانه وتعالى ينفعنا
بالعلم ويجعلنا من أهله عنده وكرمه لا رب غيره
والحمد لله وحده وصلى الله على سيدنا
محمد وآله وصحبه وسلم
ابن تمام شد في أواخر شهر
محرم الحرام سنة
أحد وثلاثين وألف

Figure 4: End of the second manuscript.

The manuscript of the Egyptian Library, Talaat collection number 790, bears the title: the Three Issues. The beginning and end of this manuscript are perfectly consistent with the Veliyuddin 1821, and it appears that Dr. Azab relied on this version as mentioned above. There are also two late copies in Berlin Library (under numbers: 2960 and 3001), which also include the issues of the Green Emerald and the Black Bead, and we were unable to check them.

As for the book of the Three Issues, there is a one-page fraction of this manuscript in the collection Ulu Cami 1619, which is described as being old.

There are also many manuscript for the book titled: "the Main Issues", which may be the mother book that includes these three issues, as we described above. However, none of these manuscripts is complete, and most of which contain only the introduction or the book's preface describing the edge of arrangement of the world. From these manuscripts we mention the collection of Yusuf Agha 4868, which appears to be written in the handwriting of the Greatest Sheikh. We have also included the beginning and end of this manuscript.

Finally, we must thank the brother Abu Ahmed, Muhammad Kaabir Al-Ansari, who provided us with some of these manuscripts in addition to the invaluable information and lengthy discussions on the origins of these interconnected books of Sheikh Muhyiddin and their various manuscripts.

The Different Names of the Single Monad:

As it may have become clear so far, the White Pearl is a designation that refers to the Single Monad (*al-jawhar al-fard*), that is the Universal Intellect itself and also the Pen, among many other names and descriptions summarized by Ibn al-Arabi this current book, and also in the first chapter of the Divine Policies for Restoring the Human Kingdom (*al-Tadbiiraat al-Ilaahiyya fi Isslaah al-Mamlakah al-Insaniyya*). There is, however, some confusion between the Greatest Element that we shall talk about shortly and the Single Monad, and sometimes it is not very clear for some of these many variant names whether they are really for the Single Monad or the Greatest

Figure 5: The beginning of Yusuf Agha 4868, which appears to be written in the handwriting of the Greatest Sheikh.

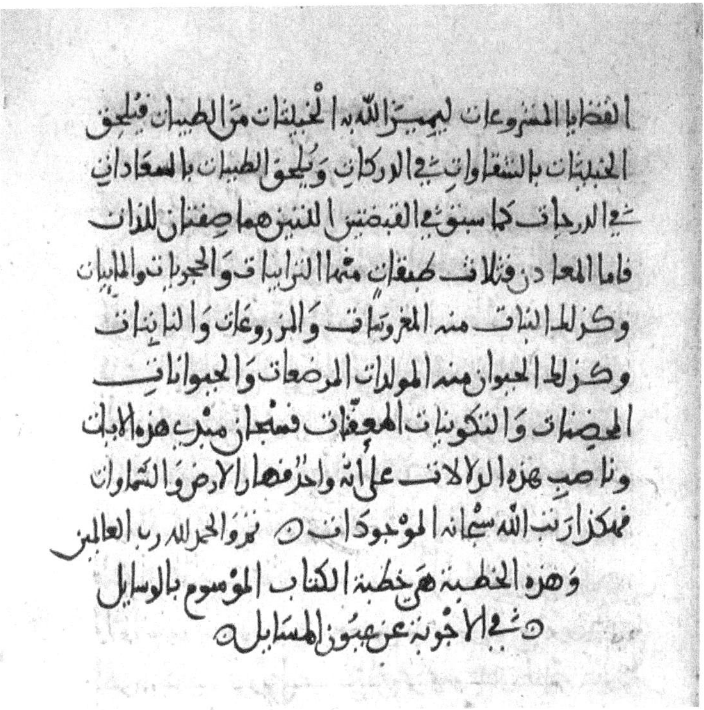

The Different Names of the Single Monad:

أفظايا المضروعات ليميّز الله به لحنيفات متى الطيبات فيلحق
الخبيثات بالسفلات نبخ الركان ويلحق الطيبات بالسعادات
نبخ الدرجات كما سبق بالقبضتين النتيز هما صفتان للذات
فاما المعادن وثلاث طبقات منها الترابيات والجبروتيات والهبائيات
وكذلك النباتات منه المعروفات والزروعات والنابتات
وكذلك الحيوان منه المولدات والرضعات والحيوانات
الحيضات والتكوينات المعفنات فسبحان مبرز هذه الذات
ونا صب هذه الولادات على اية واحد فظهار الأرض والثمرات
فتبارك رب الله سبحانه الموجودات ۞ نور الجلال رب العالمين
وهذه الخطبة هي خطبة الكتاب الموسوم بالوسايل
نبخ الأجوبة عن عيون المسايل ۞

Figure 6: The end of Yusuf Agha 4868, which appears to be written by the Greatest Sheikh.

Element.

One of these names is "the real through whom creation takes place", that is the most perfect image of the Real; Allah, the Creator of the world. That is why he is also called "the Perfect Human Being". But this name actually describes the Greatest Element rather than the Single Monad, because the latter is compound while the Greatest Element is the most elementary "block" in the world as we shall describe shortly. Everything in the Creation is rooted in the real, just as the leaves (and the fruits, ... etc) of a tree are rooted in the stalk. The leaves were also "determined" in the seed that gave this tree even before it was planted. So the Single Monad is like the seed for the tree of the cosmos, while the real-through-whom-creation-takes-place (i.e. the Greatest Element) is what makes up the seed down to the cells, atoms and subatomic particles inside it.

In his cosmological treatise "the Belt of the Restless" (*Uqlat al-Mustawfiz*), Ibn al-Arabi spoke briefly about the Greatest Element whom Allah created at once, and that's why it is conceived as indivisible and uncompounded unit, while the Single Monad, though it is an indivisible unit, is composed of or made by (or from different manifestations of) this Greatest Element.

On the other hand, in chapter 364 of the Futuhat Ibn al-Arabi talks about how the Constant Entities heard the divine Command in their state of pre-existence, thus the world moved from state of determination into real existence. He shows that there is in fact only one single entity that has a necessary immutable essence and that is the Perfect Human Being, or the Single Monad, denoted in this book as the White Pearl.

Therefore, in reality, there is only this entity that is the essence of the Perfect Human Being, and the world is the different states of this single entity, that is the Single Monad, and the essences (i.e. the monads) of the world are its different reflections, or temporal images each of which takes no more than one single instance of time, and nothing is ever repeated.

That's why another important name of the Single Monad is the Universal Spirit (*al-ruuh al-kullii*), and Ibn al-Arabi shows that he deserves this name because he goes (v. *raaha, yaruuh*) in the three conclusive states of the world, as will be detailed in the main text.

Yet another interesting name of the Single Monad is "Everything" (*kulla shay*)! This name is interesting because Ibn al-Arabi says in al-Masael that "in everything there is everything" (*kulla shayin fiihi kullu shay*), even if you do not recognize that". This is on the one hand another expression of his Single Monad theory because it renders into: "the Single Monad is in everything". But also it might mean that the internal structure of the Single Monad is as complicated as the world itself because it means: "in everything (such as the Single Monad) there is everything (such as the world)!" This statement is plausible since both the Single Monad (i.e. the Perfect Human Being) and the world are on the divine Image as we have described in the Single Monad Model.

In the Ultimate Symmetry, we showed that this essential property undermines that fractal nature of the complex-time geometry, such as Mandelbrot set, Julia set and Sierpinski triangle, where the structure keeps repeating itself on any larger or smaller scale. It just depends on the scale we are using; so if we were inside the Single Monad we might see creations such as the Sun, planets and the stars, but because we are outside we see it as a single point. Similarly, if we suppose we go outside the world, we shall see it as a single point; that is - as the Single Monad - indivisible but compound. This indeed the same as the black hole which occupies a single point in our space but itself is considered complete world.

The Oneness of Being:

These various concepts should be better understood within the frame of the Oneness of Being (*wahdata al-wujuud*). This controversial doctrine which many later Muslim scholars attributed to Ibn al-Arabi, usually with very different and often more polemic than philosophical meanings and interpretations. Although Ibn al-Arabi himself never mentioned the precise term in his writings, it is quite evident that his books are full of statements that develop notions related to the oneness of being in one way or another, in many places quite explicitly and rigorously. This is especially the case in his most controversial book, Fusus al-Hikam, for which he was widely criticized, but related discussions are also to be found throughout the Futuhat and his other shorter works.

The basic ontological issue for Ibn al-Arabi is very clear and simple: in many places throughout his writings, such as the long chapter 198 of the Futuhat [II.390-478] he follows the established Avicennan distinction in dividing all conceivable things, in terms of existence, into three basic categories: "the absolute Existence that has always been and always is (existing); and absolute (contingent) possibility (imkaan) that has always been and always is (possible to exist); and absolute non-existence that has always been and always is (non-existing)." The absolute Existence does not accept non-existence, and the absolute non-existence does not accept existence, while the absolutely possible does accept existence through a determining cause, and it also accepts non-existence through a cause. So, insofar as some of it faces non-existence, it accepts non-existence; and insofar as some of it faces Existence, it accepts existence [II.426.26]. Then he goes on to gives the crucial analysis which clearly explains his profound view of the Oneness of Being in the most explicit and direct way:

> The possible (contingent) existence became manifest between light and darkness, nature and spirit, the unseen and the visible, and the veiled and unveiled. Therefore that which is close to absolute Existence, from among all that (contingent realm) we have mentioned is light and spirit, and all of what we have mentioned which is close to absolute non-existence is shadow and body, and from the totality (of those different kinds of contingent existent) the form (of the whole of creation) comes to be. So when you consider the world from the side of the Breath of the All-Merciful, you say: It is nothing other than Allah. But when you consider the world with regard to its being equally balanced and well-proportioned (i.e., between existence and non-existence), then you say these are creations.
> ...
>
> It is through the (divine creative) Breath that the whole world is breathing (i.e. animated with life, or: moving), and the Breath made it appear. So (this creative divine Breath) is the inner dimension for the Real, and the manifest dimension for the creation: thus the inner dimension of the Real is the manifest dimension for creation, and the inner dimension of creation is the manifest aspect of the Real, and through their combination the generated existence (*al-kawn*, i.e. the Cosmos) is actualized. ... The Real is the absolute Existence, and the creation is the absolutely possible

(or potential existence). So what becomes non-existent of the world and its form that disappears is through what is close to the side of non-existence; and what remains of it and does not allow for non-existence is through what is close to the side of Existence. Hence these two things (Existence and non-existence) are continually ruling over the world, so the creation is always new with every Breath, both in this world and in the hereafter.

Therefore the Breath of the All-Merciful is continually directed (toward the Act of creation), and Nature is continually taking on existence as the forms for this Breath, so that the divine Command does not become inactive, because inactivity is not appropriate (for It). So constantly forms are newly appearing and becoming manifest, according to their states of readiness to accept the (divine creative) Breath. And this is the clearest possible (description) of the (divine) origination of the world. And Allah says the truth and He shows the way (Quran, 33:4). [II.427.17]

This expression implies that the world can be conceived symbolically as a mixture of light and darkness. However, darkness is quite literally nothing: it is simply the absence of light. Light, on the other hand, is ultimately the Real (via the divine Name the Light: *al-nuur*), and the Real is One. So all existence is in essence one. Multiplicity appears through creation as a result of mixing the oneness of light with the darkness of non-existence.

In other words, since darkness is nothing, the creation is the constantly repeating relative appearance (manifestation) of the Real.

The Real manifests most perfectly in the Perfect Human Being, and relatively in other creatures, and these manifestations happen through the Universal Intellect. So in real existence there is only the Real Who is Allah and this Universal Intellect who is the Messenger of Allah.

This is the basic principle in Ibn al-Arabi's cosmology, but in order to understand it we need to explain how exactly the mixing between light and darkness is taking place, which raises the question of time. Therefore, these essential concepts have been developed into the Single Monad Model and Duality of Time Theory, as we shall briefly describe below to make this book more easily accessible to readers. However, a full description of that is present in the three volumes of the Single Monad Model book series.

The Single-Monad Model:

Based in the Oneness of Being, the Single Monad Model of the Cosmos was proposed in

2005, and developed further and published in 2007 and 2014. According to this model, the Cosmos is being dynamically created (or re-created) from one single metaphysical entity that is sequentially generating the physical dimensions and what they may contain of matter particles.

The Single Monad Model can be summarized in the following three hypotheses:

1. **The Single Monad**: At any instance of time, of the real flow of time, there is only one Single Monad that alone can be described with real existence. This Monad creates other monads by manifesting in different forms, thus imaging itself to make a comprehensive image as one single frame of the entire cosmos. This still picture is created in one full Week of the original creative Days of events (described further in Chapter IV of the Duality of Time), but this creative process is equivalent only to one single moment for an observer inside the Cosmos.

2. **The Re-creation Principle**: The forms of manifestation of the Single Monad

cease to exist intrinsically right after the instance of their creation, and then they are **re-created** again by the Single Monad in every original creative Week, equivalent to one instance of our normal time. This perpetual re-creation happens in the "six Days" of creation from Sunday to Friday, which accounts for the three dimensions of space, but we don't witness this creation process. Instead, we only witness an instance of the created world on the "last Day" of Saturday, as time. So the seven Days of the divine Week are one abstract geometrical point of space-time, which then form the space-time container that encompasses the world both spatially and temporally.

3. **The Actual Flow of Time**: Since the world takes seven Days to be created by the Single Monad, which manifests the forms of the individual monads one by one in specific order, the observers would be out of existence for six Days, from Sunday to Friday, before they witness the next moment of creation, that is the next frame of space, on the following

Saturday, but we perceive all this as a single discrete moment, as we described above. In each Day of these Days of creation, a corresponding dimension of the world is created. Therefore, the real flow of the actual created time doesn't go linearly, but it is intertwined with the observable, normal earthly days in the special and rather mystifying manner that has been summarized in Chapter IV of the Volume I of the Single Monad Model book series.

This extremely complex view of space-time and creation lead to the Duality of Time hypothesis which was able to explain many persisting philosophical and cosmological problems in terms of the genuinely-complex time-time geometry. This theory was developed in the second volume of the Single Monad Model, published in 2017.

The Duality of Time Theory:

The Duality of Time Postulate states that: *at every instance of the outward normal level of time, space and matter are perpetually being re-created in one linear chronological sequence, which forms the inward levels of time that are also nested inside each lower dimension of space.*

This means that at every instance of the real flow of time there is only one metaphysical point, that is the unit of space-time geometry, and the Universe is a result of its perpetual recurrence in the inner levels of time, which is continuously and perpetually re-creating the dimensions of space and what it may contain of matter particle, which then kinetically evolve throughout the outer normal level of time that we encounter.

With regard to observers who are habitually living in the normal level of time, the process of re-creation is instantaneous, since it is performed by a massless metaphysical point, that is always moving at the speed of light, which is the only real speed in nature. Mass, energy and other physical properties, including velocity, acceleration and even the dimensions of matter and space, are only observable on the outward (imaginary) level of time, as a result of the temporal coupling between at least two metaphysical points or instances.

This metaphysical entity, that forms the unit of space-time geometry, is the Single Monad, or the Universal Intellect, that is the White Pearl; among some other names and descriptions summarized by Ibn al-Arabi in the current book. The discrete points of space are the temporal forms or individual temporary monads that occur through its perpetual recurrence in the inner levels of time which is dynamically creating the physical multiplicity, that then evolve on the outer level.

This single postulate leads at the same time to all the three principles of Special and General Relativity together, as well as Quantum Field Theory, including the first and second quantization, of energy and fields, and hence this "third quantization" of space-time itself, which will eliminate all kinds of infinities that are normally encountered in the current background continuum models, due to singularities in the ill-defined Riemannian geometry.

In Volumes II and III of the Single Monad Model, we explained how the Duality of Time can solve many, if not all, of the major problems in physics and cosmology, including: the

Arrow of Time, the Problem of Physical Information, the Problem of Causality, the Planck Scale, the existence of the Magnetic Monopole, the EPR and the Problem of Non-Locality, Quantum Gravity, Mass Generation Mechanism, Homogeneity and the Horizon Problem, the Hierarchy Problem, Super-Symmetry and Matter-Antimatter Asymmetry, in addition to the problem of Dark Matter and Dark Energy, and the Cosmological Constant. Many of these problems will be simply eliminated according to the new genuinely-complex time-time geometry.

What is the Single Monad:

Borrowing his language from the atomist physical theories of earlier *kalam* theology, Ibn al-Arabi sometimes refers to the created world as being made up of monads and forms, or in his technical language, of "substances" (*jawaahir*, s. *jawhar*) and various changing "accidents" (*aaraad*, s. *aarad*) that inhere in and qualify those substances. In the process of manifestation, the substances appear to remain relatively constant, while the accidents do not stay for more than one moment. In this terminology, the "monad" or substance (*al-jawhar*) is a metaphysical entity that exists by itself, whereas the "form" or accident (*al-aarad*) exists only through or by some particular monad. The monad, however, may appear in existence only by "wearing" some form or another [II.179.26], so we only observe the forms, rather than the monads. Also Ibn al-Arabi asserts that the monad exists by itself and its existence is constant and invariable, while the form exists only in or through the monad and its existence is temporal; it only exists at the time and then it vanishes instantly and intrinsically, and the same never comes back to existence again [II.677.30, III.452.24].

Generally, *jawhar* signifies everything that exists in reality. Literally it originally meant "jewel", but in this technical sense borrowed from the physical theory of *kalam* theology, it means "substance".

In English, the word "monad" is derived from the Greek *monados*, and it means "ultimate, indivisible unit". It was used very early by the Greek philosophers of the doctrines of Pythagoras, and it was also used later, in a very different way, by the neo-Platonists to signify the One: thus God is described as the "Monad of monads".

Like the neo-Platonists, Ibn al-Arabi sometimes uses this term in this higher theological sense to refer to "the one", "the essence", "the real" (but not "the Real" as a divine Name of God, but "the real-through-whom-creation-takes-place", as discussed further in this book). However, in such cases he does not employ this term to refer directly to the highest, transcendent dimension of "God", but rather to the Universal Intellect, who is also the "Perfect Human Being".

The Structure of the Monad:

Ibn al-Arabi is well aware that there has long been a debate amongst philosophers whether the monad is a physical or metaphysical entity, or whether it is embodied or not. At the beginning of the first chapter of al-Tadbiiraat al-Ilaahiyya, Ibn al-Arabi says: "The first existent originated by Allah is a simple spiritual single monad, embodied according to some doctrines and not-embodied according to others ..." (Tadbiiraat: 87, see also [Futuhat, I.47.22]).

Although he mostly prefers the second opinion, as it will be clarified in this book, he sometimes does not rule out either case, perhaps because the argument should be meaningless, i.e. the reality must necessarily encompass all manifestations of creation, both spiritual and manifest, if we recall that there is in reality only one Single Monad. Many times, though, he affirms that the Single Monad is embodied and indivisible, especially when the manifest world is concerned [II.438.2].

On the other hand, the essences of the spirits and souls are not likely to be embodied [II.309.25], though both (the manifest and spiritual) are only reflections of the Single Monad that itself can neither be described as (solely) physical nor as metaphysical, because it is necessarily the whole of creation.

In the very long chapter 198 of the Futuhat, in which Ibn al-Arabi talks in detail about the various aspects of divine creation, he summarizes the various divisions or types of physical and metaphysical entities. He also states the difference between the essences (monads) and their accidents (forms).

The Greatest Element:

As we have explained with more details in the Single Monad Model, although the Single Monad is an indivisible unit, it is understood to be composed of even more elementary constituents that somehow underlie and help manifest the monads, even though the monad itself is not physically divisible into those metaphysical constituents, but can only exist in manifestation as a substance created through those underlying constituents. This ultimate constituent of the Single Monad is called the Greatest Element (*al-unsuur al-aazam*).

In his book Uqlat al-Mustawfiz, Ibn al-Arabi explains that Allah created the "Greatest Element" in the "Absolute Unseen" which may not be disclosed to any creature. He also indicates there that the creation or "origination" of this Greatest Element is all at once, without any intermediate or associated causes. So this original, metaphysical Greatest Element that is in some mysterious way the substrate of all subsequent manifest creation—whether purely spiritual, imaginal, or physical — is the only thing that in some way underlies, constitutes, or gives rise to the physical monads. The individual monad, however, remains the basic indivisible structure in the physically manifest world.

The resulting relation between the manifest world, the Single Monad (First Intellect) and the Greatest Element can be conceived by analogy to the relation between a building, the bricks and the clay: i.e., the building is made up of similar unit bricks, but the brick itself is made from fine clay.

Ibn al-Arabi affirms that this Greatest Element is the most perfect thing in existence and that everything other than Allah is somehow derived from it. However, he does not give much information about It, and he even says that he would explain the reality of this Element if he was not sworn not to disclose it.

In the summary cosmological chapter 60 of the Futuhat, Ibn al-Arabi alludes more symbolically, in a metaphysical exegesis of Quran 68:1 ("Nuun and the Pen, and what they are inscribing"), to the Greatest Element when he speaks of the mysterious figure of "Nuun" whom Allah appointed as the divine "chamberlain" (*al-haajib*) and gave all His Knowledge of His creation, so that Allah - with regard to His Name "the All-Knowing" — never hides from the Nuun. And Allah appointed another angel, the Pen - who is the Single Monad, First Intellect, Perfect Human Being, etc. — as the "scribe" for the Nuun, "writing out" all of the divine Knowledge of His creation [I.294.33].

The White Pearl in the Other Books

As we noted above, Ibn al-Arabi mentioned the name "the White Pearl" several times in his other books, such as Uqlat al-Mustawfiz and the Meccan Revelations. In fact, throughout all his books, the Greatest Master offered detailed analysis of his ontological views of creation, involving many key statements on the various names and descriptions of the White Pearl, though he might not mention this name directly, but other terms such as the Universal Intellect or the Perfect Human.

In his answer to the questions of al-Hakim al-Tirmidhi, Sheikh Muhyiddin says:

If you say: "What is the (Black) Bead?" We say: "It is

the Chaos (*hiyola*), in which are initiated the bodies of the world that was originated from the Green Emerald." Then if you say: "What is the Green Emerald?" We say: "It is the Soul that emanated from the White Pearl." Then if you say: "What is the White Pearl?" We say: "it is the First Intellect." [Futuhat, II.130].

He also said in his introduction to the Meccan Revelations:

> In the First Book of Knowledge (*Kitab al-Maerifa al-Awwal*), we totaled the aspects of knowledge that the Intellect has in the world, and we did not mention from where we got that limitation! Thus you should know that the Intellect has three hundred and sixty facets, each of which corresponds to three hundred and sixty aspects from the cherished Real; and each aspect gives (specific) knowledge that the others do not give. So if you multiply the facets of the Intellect with the aspects of reception; the result gives the (kinds of) knowings of the Intellect, that are inscribed in the Protected Tablet, that is the Soul. [Futuhat: I.46]

Moreover, in this book of Knowledge, mentioned above, otherwise also called the Issues (*al-Masael*), Ibn al-Arabi gives a short list of the various names and descriptions of the White Pearl:

> The first confined and limited existent to appear is called "the First Intellect", and he is called "the Universal Spirit" and he is called "the Pen", and he is called "Just" and he is called "the Throne" and he is called "the Real-through-which-things-are-created", and he is called "the Mohammedan Reality", and he is called "the Spirit of the Spirits", and is called "the

Clear Leader", and he is called "Everything", among many names according to his various aspects.

On the other hand, from one point of view, this Intellect is (fashioned) according to the half of the (divine) Image that we know, based on narration and revealing, but also according to the whole Image, from another view; depending what is manifesting. The whole world is created according to the Image, and the Human with relation to this world is created according to the image of the world, so it is on the (same) Image (or the image of the Image). Spiritual beings are steadier in perfection than the world of objects, for their fullest readiness, and that's why human beings are naturally inclined to attaining spiritual power. Hence, some of them achieved perfection, and some of them did not reach due to some accidental and inherent barriers in this (lower) world. But in the Hereafter, all shall come to achieve it, but the privilege then lies among them in other things that are due to the (specific) image in which they enter.

When this first being was created, he got three hundred and sixty faces towards the Divine Presence, so that the Real emanated on him from His knowledge according to his preparation for acceptance. Thus, his acceptance was forty-six thousand thousands (i.e. millions) and six hundred and sixty fifty thousand (because he has three main aspects, so this number is: 360 x 360 x 360 = 46,656,000).

[the Issues, Issue No. 10 in the edition of Dar al-Kutub al-Ilmiyya, 2001, p.307]

Then in Uqlat al-Mustawfiz the Sheikh explained how the First Intellect receives the divine knowledge though his three-hundred and sixty faces we just mentioned above:

The thing that Allah created in the world of the managing intellects is a simple substance (or: monad), that is not material, nor being confined in matter. He knows himself, by himself. His knowledge is his own self. He has no (further) description. His station is poverty and humiliation, and the need for his Creator, originator and Inventor. He has some proportions and additions, and many faces, but he does not multiply in himself when he multiplies. He emanates in two ways: self-emanation and voluntary emanation. The absolute self-emanation is not characterized by deterrence, but that which is voluntary can be described by prevention and giving. Yet he is essentially subjected to his Creator, the Almighty, from Whom he gained his existence. Allah called him in Quran: "the Real (through whom creation takes place)", "the Pen" and "the Spirit", and in the Hadith (it is called) "the Intellect", among other names that we have mentioned in many of our books.

... And his connections that extend to the Soul, to the Chaos, to the Body, to the fixed orbs, to the center, to the pillars, then by ascending to the disseminating orbs, to the movements, to the generators, to the human, and then to their joining in the Greatest Element that is their origin, are: forty-six thousand thousands (i.e. millions) and six hundred and sixty fifty thousand connection.

This Intellect is still alternating between facing and turnout, so he faces his Originator to accept the knowledge through the manifestation that reveals to him some of his states, so he becomes aware of his Creator as much as he knew of himself; but since his knowledge of himself is not finite, so his knowledge in his Lord is not finite. He knows himself though the manifestations, and he knows his Lord as he knows himself. Then he turns out to face what is below to give them the knowledge. Always like that, for eternity, always growing. Thus, he is the rich and the poor, the dear and the humble, the master and the slave. The Real is still inspiring to request for manifestations to collect more knowledge.

[Uqlat al-Mustawfiz, The Section of the Intellect]

He also said in the same book of Uqlat al-Mustawfiz:

When Allah, the Almighty, created the Highest Pen, He created for him - in the second station - the Soul, that is the Protected Tablet, ... and He ordered the Pen to flow on this Tablet with what was He estimated and ordained of that to be created. ... Therefore, this Tablet is the place of intellectual depositing, just as Eve with relation to Adam, peace be upon him. She was called Soul (nafes) because she was found from the Breath (nafas) of the Merciful, So Allah relieved the Intellect with her by making her a place to accept what he is delivering and a tablet of what he is inscribing.

... This Pen has three hundred and sixty heads, in terms of his being a pen, and three hundred and sixty faces and proportion in terms of his being an intellect, and three hundred sixty tongues in terms of his being a spirit translating from Allah. Each head of the three hundred and sixty is drawing from three hundred and sixty seas, which are classes of science, and they were called seas because of their breadth. These seas are the sum of the (divine) Words that do not run out ... This holy angel (that is the Tablet or the Soul) has two aspects; a luminous one from the side of the holy Intellect, and a dark one from the side that follows the Chaos, the sea of Nature, thus she is in herself green for this amazing and delicate combination. We have mentioned this in the Book of the Soul, which is the Book of the Green Emerald, and we also mentioned the station of the Highest Pen in a separate book called "the White Pearl".

The following is the full text of the White Pearl (*al-Durrat al-Bayda*), by the Greatest Master Muhyiddin Ibn Al-Arabi, may Allah be pleased with him. The comments and other explanations between brackets are added by the translator.

Note: In addition to the footnotes, all comments between (normal) or [medium] brackets are added by the translator. This is also the case for punctuation and all section titles, in the Arabic and English versions. Schematic figures are also added to demonstrate the Single Monad Model and Duality of Time Theory. Some of these figures are borrowed from the previous volumes in the Single Monad Model book series.

The White Pearl (by the Greatest Master Muhyiddin Ibn al-Arabi)

[Introduction:]

In the Name of Allah, the All-Compassionate and the All-Merciful.

In Him is my trust.

[The Self-Existence of Allah:]

You should know that Allah, the Praised and the Exalted, is the Absolute Being, not after nonexistence. His Existence is necessary for Himself. He has always been existing, and He has always been One in His Essence.

To Him belong the Beautiful Names and the Lofty Descriptions. Yet He is not multiplied through (the multiplicity of) His Names and Descriptions. That who is one in his essence doesn't multiply by the meanings that are recognized in him, because the stand-alone essence may (only) be multiplied if it accepts division; i.e. if it is composed of parts, or it is subject to counting. But the descriptions are not part of that which is described by them.

Moreover, He, the Exalted, is not substance, nor in-substance, but He is Independent, Self-standing, not-embodied, and He is not subject to incidents.

His Existence is proved (certain), and no other essence is (really) existing other than Him.

Everything other than Him exists by Him, it is done by Him, created by Him, and made by Him.

[**Potential Existence:**]

The existence of what exists (in the World) is conditioned upon His Will (*iraada*), that is His Wish (*mashiaa*) - the Exalted - and His Ability (*qudra*), and His Knowledge (*ilm*).

This dependent (i.e. the potential, or contingent, or Possible) existence may only be (conceived of that it has become) after non-existence, otherwise it wouldn't be a "possible", as it is in the matter of fact, and it

[Potential Existence:] 51

wouldn't be an existence (created) by this Necessary (*al-waajib*), while it is (in fact) an existence created by Him.

What He (the creator) did is to cause its essence to exist, which means that it is (always) in need of Allah, the Exalted, to bring it into existence. (Even after it is brought into existence, it is still always in need of the Creator, because its existence - since it is not necessary - may not persist for more than one instance. So it is always in need to be brought into existence, at every instance of time.)

However, this need is not for his (very) essence, because his immutable essence (existed in eternity and it) isn't determined by any determiner; because there is no determination in eternity.[2]

---

[2] Ibn al-Arabi always affirms that the entities had a special state of pre-existence in the fore-knowledge of Allah even before He creates them. This pre-existence is eternal because it is itself the knowledge of Allah that is not other than Him, Who is Eternal. This subject was discussed at length in the book of Eternity, that is Volume II of this series.

Then he, may Allah exalt his *Sirr*[3], said:[4]

[The Becoming of the World:]

Therefore, the existence of the Possible can only be after its non-existence, which means that it was not and then it is (so it has a beginning in time), because the reality of the Possible is that it doesn't resist becoming into existence like the Impossible (that is the absolute non-existence, such as a squared circle or another god with Allah), nor into the non-existence like the necessary (that is the absolute Existence, nothing but Allah). But, it is possible if it is existing to de-exist, and it is possible if it was non-existing to exist.

---

[3] *Sirr*, in Arabic means "secret", but the Sufis use this word to describe the face of the heart that is the place of the manifestation of Allah. This face in relation to the heart is like the heart in relation to the soul, so it is the heart of the heart. And this *Sirr* also has a *Sirr*, and it might go like that to seven levels, and some even say nine.

[4] It is clear from this sentence that this book may have been written by some students of Ibn al-Arabi, maybe based on his response to a question he was asked about the First Intellect, as the full (Arabic) title also indicates. This will be even more obvious in the last few sentences by which this book is ended. Therefore, the style of the book is an oral speech, and for this reason it is very hard to decide where to put the correct punctuation to start, divide and end the sentences, specially for such a profound and sensitive philosophical subject.

[The Becoming of the World:]

Thus, it necessarily needs a preponderator (*murajjih*).

This preponderator cannot be "possible" like it, since this (founding) possible requires a preponderator (on its own, and so on in endless series). This is also impossible because the non-existent (that is the initial state of the possible existence) doesn't preponderate anything (because nothing may ever come from nothing, or we can also say that: the Possible does not have any intrinsic ability, as the author shall explain further below.).

Therefore, the preponderator has to be necessarily-existing for itself, and He is (nothing but) Allah, the Praised.

Also this Possible cannot be necessarily-existing by Allah, the Exalted, otherwise it would be with Him eternally, and the existence of the Possible is impossible to be eternal, because there will be no use of the necessarily existent if it wasn't after non-existence.

The reality of the Possible doesn't accept the (absolute) conceptual necessity, nor the dependent necessity that is called "necessary by other".

On the other hand, it is not possible for the

"Will" to relate to something that is (already) existing, but it (always) relates to the non-existent (in order to bring it into existence). If the Will is (thought to be) related to the endurance (or continuity) of what is existing, this will not happen, because its existence (that may look to be endured continuously) is (in fact) always occurring (anew).[5]

The Possible is that whose existence and non-existence are equally imaginable, without any preponderance for itself, because if it preponderates the existence on non-existence by itself, this either happen when it is existing or when it is non-existing. If it preponderates its existence while it exists, then what did it preponderate? And it is impossible to preponderate its existence while it is non-existing, because the non-existent is not a thing, so no rule may be logically expected out of it.

Therefore, if we see the Possible has been preponderated into one of the two possibilities (that are: becoming into existence if it was not existing, or becoming into nonexistence

---

[5]This statement follows from the re-creation principle, one of the three principles of the Single Monad Model. This means that nothing can remain the same in existence for more than one instance of time, and nothing is ever repeated twice.

if it was existing, then), we know that this was the result of the Will of its preponderator, who has to be necessarily-existent and who wills to give existence to this possible.

On the other hand, the necessarily-existing is that whose non-existence is not imaginable in logic, just as the existence of the (impossible that is absolutely) non-existent is also not imaginable in logic.

[**The Re-creation of the World:**]

It doesn't follow (from the previous statements which imply) that the Will (of the preponderator) is necessarily-existing (since it is an attribute of the Creator, Who is Necessarily-existing), (it doesn't follow that) when it relates to the Possible (to bring it into existence), that it must have been always with it (described by eternity) since the Will is eternal; this is not necessary. (So the Will is an eternal description of the Creator, but relating it to the Possible is not.)

It has been proved that the Will doesn't relate to other than what is non-existing (at the time), so if the non-existent became into existence the Will would no more be related to it by the fact that it is existing, because non-existence has already been proved to it (since it is only possible to exist), but - at the time of its existence - it may relate (to it only) with respect to the continuity of its existence, (so it relates to it in fact only) when it is non-existent (because it is being re-created at every instance), and it is (being) extincted (or deceased) in the second time, whether assumed time (for incorporeal entities) or real time (for physical entities), whichever time that is, though the essence is existing (but the form is being always re-created in it).

Therefore, every possibly-existing is only (always becoming into existence) after non-existence (and not continuously existing).

This is also true for the Ability (as an eternal description of the Creator); its relation to existence ceases (as soon as it becomes), because it (only) relates to it in order to bring it into existence, then no more relation to this existence other than creating the (ever-new) forms by which its endurance is fulfilled, so they are being renewed on it.

That's why the Creator (*al-baarii*), the Praised, is Always-Creator (*Khallaaq*) in this world and in the hereafter. (Otherwise, if something is repeated twice the same, He would be limited.)

[**The Single Monad:**]

Then you should know that when Allah, the Exalted, created this Intellect, that is a Single Monad, self-standing, embodied according to some doctrines and not embodied according to others - which is more accurate - He manifested to him, thus He emanated on him all the knowable things. (This conclusion comes from the Hadith Ibn al-Arabi always cite in this regard, that "the first of what Allah created was the Pen; then He created the Tablet and said unto the Pen: write!, so the Pen said: what to write? Then Allah said unto him: you write and I shall dictate you. [*Kanz*: 15116]. So the Pen, that is the Single Monad, is writing in the Tablet what Allah is dictating to him, which is His Knowledge regarding His creation that He shall create till the resurrection Day [*Futuhat*: I.139.23].)

This means that his knowledge has (already) been related to all knowable things (so his knowledge with relation to the Creation is complete), but his knowledge of Allah, the Exalted, is not (complete) because he never encompasses knowing Him [*Quran*: 20.110], but Allah, the Exalted, is still always emanating knowledge on him and he is still accepting.

This is why he is described by "finding out", not with respect to the cosmological knowledge, since he (already) knew it all, but it is impossible that he absolutely knows Allah, the Exalted.

Prophet Muhammad, may Allah have mercy and peace upon him, referred to this fact by saying: "*I ask You by every Name that is for You, those You named Yourself with, those You taught to anyone of Your Creation, or those You alone possessed in Your hidden knowledge*" [*Kanz*: 3434, 3435, 3436]. So his saying "*or You alone possessed!*" is what we meant (that the names of Allah, and thus His manifestations, are never ending, and cannot be encompassed by anyone).

[**Some of the Names of the Single Monad:**]

And this existent (that is the Intellect) has different names and designations:

[The Intellect:]

Some of them (i.e. the Sufis and other knowledgeable scholars) called him "**the Intellect**" (*al-aql*)[6] (and that's from the following narration, where) the Prophet, may Allah have mercy and peace upon him, said: *"The first of what Allah has created is the Intellect, then He said unto him: come forth! Thus he came forward, and then He said unto him: turn away! So he turned away [Kanz: 7058].* So he came forward to benefit and turned away to give out.

However, his turning away is (actually) coming forward, because the (divine) Name that said unto him: come forward - and then he came forward - and then another Name said unto him turn away - so he turned away - thus he was taken by another Name (so he is always coming forward towards his Originator, but to different divine Names, and that's what causing the different never-ending manifestations that never repeat the same at all!).

(We showed in the Ultimate Symmetry

---

[6] Ibn al-Arabi also calls the Single Monad: the First / Universal Intellect as we have seen in the Single Monad Model.

that the points of the absolute space, at the level ultimate symmetry, which are commonly known in Islamic mysticism as the Constant Entities; we showed that they are described by the property of spin, which then bring them down to the level of hyper-symmetry, before this latter breaks through super-symmetry into the physical and psychical worlds. The author is clearly alluding to that, as it may become more clear in the following. Only we need to remember that all the points of space are different forms, or individual monads, of the Single Monad Monad, that is the Universal Intellect we are describing here.)

Therefore, in this fundamental structure (that he was built on) he was given (the two properties of) coming forward and turning away, because the (whole) existence is built upon them, and these are the two fists (*Qabddatayn*, s. *Qabddah*), and the two facts that rule over the World with happiness and misery. From this coming forward and turning away, the Paradise and Hell appeared; the grasping and release, the pain and the pleasure, the non-existence and existence, so there is only the duality, and anything above two

[Some of the Names of the Single Monad:]

is necessarily reduced to this duality, if you examine it carefully. Even the three and others. You should know that! (For example, the fundamental trinity of the cosmos - that's the subject, object, and act - is in fact two, because the act is only the connection or the isthmus between them. But also you should know that the two is in fact nothing but the one, because they are like the matching names of the first and the last, the manifest and the hidden, and so on. So in reality there is only one that's taking the role of the three, but not at the same time, as we have seen in the Duality of Time Theory.)

The whole existence is confined in the reality of "grasping" (that come after: "releasing"[7]), and that's why the Prophet, may Allah have mercy and peace upon him, came out with the two books (i.e. Quran and Sunnah), and also all realities are confined in: attribute and attributed, there is nothing but it has a matching opposite.

---

[7]This can be compared to what Ibn al-Arabi has already said in the Book of Eternity (*azal*), that's volume II of this series, that the World is always vanishing by the manifestation of the *alif* from *azal*.

[The Pen:]

Some of them called him "**the Pen**" (*al-qalam*):[8]

the Exalted (Allah) said: *(by the) Nuun, and the Pen* [*Quran*: 68.1], and the Prophet, may Allah have mercy and peace upon him, said: *"The first that Allah, the Exalted, created is the Pen, and He (then) created (for him, from his shadow) the Tablet, and said unto him: "write", so he said: "O Lord, what shall I write?", which indicates his limitation and needfullness, "so his Lord, the Exalted, said unto him: "write My Knowledge in My Creation till the resurrection day." so the Pen flowed with what, the Exalted, ordered him"* [*Kanz*: 597, 15116, 15117, 15118, 15220, 15223].

This means that the Pen was already taught (all what he shall write, by the first manifestation) by Allah, but he only stopped because he didn't know which kind (of knowledge) he should write of the kinds of knowledge that he had been taught. So, when this was specified, he flowed according to what he already knew. (This point is important, because it means

---

[8]Ibn al-Arabi also calls him the First / Higher Universal Pen.

that although everything is predestined by Allah, the Pen, or the Single Monad, what he should be specifically writing at the time. Otherwise ...) If he didn't need any knowledge originally, what is then the benefit of the continuing emanation on him, and his everlasting continuity![9]

Then you should know that, despite this (high) state of knowledge, he is (still) seeking his Lord just as you seek Him, but according to his (high) potential in which Allah configured him, not according to your (limited) potential (as a partial intellect, or individual monad).

[The Universal Spirit:]

Some of them called him "**the Universal Spirit**" (*al-ruuh al-kull*):

Allah, the Exalted, mentioned: *so, when I have made him and have breathed into him of*

---

[9]It seems from this brief description that although everything was taught to the Intellect when Allah manifested unto him, this Single Monad needs to stop - at various levels - to ask God what he should be writing at the time. Indeed this process itself is what causes time, otherwise if the Single Monad writes everything at once there will be no succeeding causes and results, and no events confined in time, but only one transcendental spatial dimension.

My Spirit ... [*Quran*: 15.29], so He added the Spirit to Him by way of honor, not that it is the soul of the Exalted Creator.

Also, the Exalted, said (to His Prophet Muhammad peace be upon him): *say: the Spirit is from the Command of my Lord* [*Quran*: 17.85]. This indicates that he (i.e. the Universal Spirit, or the Single Monad) is seeking Allah out of passion (since he belongs to Him).[10]

The reason why he is designated as "Universal" (*kullii*) is because all the states of the World are confined in it. They emerge out of him and return back to him, and he is the first cause to create all the essences and the spirits.

He deserved this name from two aspects; the first is for his being a spirit, i.e. in ease, happiness, and rest (*raaha* p.p. of *yastariih*; to rest or to relieve) due to his knowledge of his Lord and his witnessing Him.

The second is that he went (*raaha*, past

---

[10]From here comes "the Principle of Love" as the fundamental cause of "motion", as we described in the Ultimate Symmetry. We also showed that this principle leads to the known principle of Least Action, which is the primary assumption in most modern physics theories, including Relativity and Quantum theories.

[Some of the Names of the Single Monad:]

tense of *yaruuh*; to go) through the capacious orbs of the knowledge of his Creator, by a special force. And he went through the states of the cosmos to give out to it what Allah entrusted him. And he went through his knowing himself by his need to his Lord and his Creator.

So he has three goings (*rawahaat*, hence his three main aspects mentioned below) so he may be called "Universal Spirit" because there is no fourth state other than those to go through.

Also, (this name is derived from the fact that) it is like the imperative (tense) of "*raaha*" (went): "*yaruuhu*" (is the past participle, go) and the imperative is "*ruh*" (go!); and when it was transformed from the imperative to the noun, the "*waaw*" was returned to it as also the "*alif*" and "*lam*" (of the definitive article) were added, because the omitting of "*waaw*" from it was due to the meeting of the two consonants,[11]

So it is like: whenever he was sought from one direction then it is said that he has gone

---

[11] In Arabic grammar when two consonant characters meet one of them is omitted, usually the vowel.

(*raaha*), as we said.

[The Real-Through-Whom-Creation-Takes-Place:]

Some of them called him "**the real through whom creation takes place**" ("*al-haqq al-makhluuq bihi*").

This name was adopted by some scholars, such as Abu al-Hakam bin Barrajaan[12].

This name is derived from the saying of Allah, the Cherished and the Glorified: *We created them but only with the real* [*Quran*: 44.39], and, the Exalted, also said: *with the real We have sent it down, and with the real it has descended* [*Quran*: 17.105], and His saying: *We created not the Heavens and the Earth and all that is between them save with the real* [*Quran*: 15.85].

However, he (i.e. bin Burrajaan) called him "the real through whom creation takes

---

[12] Abu-l-Hakam Abd al-Salam ibn Abd al-Rahman ibn Mohammad ibn Barrajan was born in Seville, and he lived there to become one of the greatest Sufi figures of Andalus, and also a hadith scholar. He is most famous for his prediction of the opening of Quds by Salahudeen Ayyubi. His writings had a great influence on Ibn al-Arabi. He died in Marrakesh in 1141 AD.

[Some of the Names of the Single Monad:]

place" because "the Real" is a Name of Allah, the Exalted, and is not created.

The meaning of "creating" (here) is "making it existing after being non-existing", or also "estimating", and both are adequate (descriptions) for him (so, we can that everything is created or estimated by the real, either way is correct).

[The Just:]

Some of them called him "**the Just**" (*al-adl*).

This was adopted by Abu Ubaid-Allah Sahl ibn Abd-Allah al-Tustari[13], who quoted the narration that: the Heavens and the Earth are held by the Just.

Allah, the Exalted, said: *Observe the measure strictly* [*Quran*: 55.9], which is (nothing but) "justice", "*With the Real have We sent it down*", i.e. justice.

And he is the first to accept the form of the Just (that is one of the Beautiful Names of Allah) because he departed (*adala*) from

---

[13] Sahl al-Tustari (c.818 CE / 203 AH) – c.896 CE / 283 AH), was a Persian Muslim scholar and early classical Sufi mystic. He is most famous for his controversial claim that "I am the Proof of God", and for his well-known Quran commentary and interpretation.

his self to his Creator, the Exalted.

[The Clear Register, and the Preserved Tablet:]

Some of them called him "**the Clear Register**" (**al-imaam al-mubiin**) and "**the Preserved Tablet**" (**al-lawh al-mahfuuz**).

Allah, the Exalted, said: *and all things We have enumerated in a Clear Register* [*Quran*: 36.12]. This existent (that is the Single Monad) is the one in whom He enumerated everything.

(On the other hand) Allah, the Exalted, said: *Nay, but it is a glorious Quran, in a Preserved Tablet* [*Quran*: 85.21-22]. So this existent is a "tablet", since the Real wrote (or enumerated) everything in him, and he is "preserved" because the contents do not change.

However, other groups said that the Tablet is the Soul, while this (Single Monad) is the Pen (as described above), and as we shall explain shortly if Allah, the Exalted, wills.

[Other Names:]

There are many other descriptions (for the Single Monad), that may only be enumerated

[The Eternal Existence of Allah:] 69

by their Creator. In general, everyone considered a specific property in him, so they called him by a name based on such consideration.[14]

[The Eternal Existence of Allah:]

Therefore, the Praised Creator is (described as) the Old, the Eternal, the Knowing, the Willing, the Able Whom no possible (existence) may resist (being the subject of) his Ability (to bring into existence), while He is the (absolute) Existent (or: Being), not after non-existence.

He is Enduring by Himself, and He is described by absolute Completeness, and realized Perfectness.

[The Temporal Existence of the Intellect:]

On the other hand, as for this existent that is the Intellect, his (becoming into) existence

---

[14]In addition to the above names, the author also mentioned in *Uqlat al-Mustawfiz* and in *al-Tadbiiraat al-Ilaahiyya* many other names, such as: "**the First Matter**", "**the First Teacher**", "**the Throne**", "**the Mirror of the Real and Reality**", "**the Emanator (*al-mufiidh*)**" and "**the Centre of the Circle**". Also, in "*Al-Tanazzulaat al-Layliyya fi al-Ahkaam al-Ilaahiyya*" and other books, he adds to the previous: "**the Muhammadan Reality**", "**the Spirit of Spirits**" and "**Everything**", as we also mentioned in the Introduction.

is conditioned by (his original) non-existence. So his existence is subject to the (Divine) Wish. He was not, and then he is. From the moment of his essence was created, he is still accepting the divine emanation, and the generosity descending through the subtle Unseen (*ghayb*).

[**The Perpetual Emanation:**]

The emanation of Allah, the Exalted, cannot be imagined to held (or obscured), contracted, or ended. However, it varies according to the acceptors; so it is light for the luminous, darkness for the dark, color in the colored, motion in the moving, knowledge in the knowing, will in the willing, and preservation in the preserved.

[**Divine Generosity:**]

You should understand what we have indicated; because if there is any contraction towards any existent, the name of generosity (for the divine) wouldn't be more appropriate than greed. Therefore, whoever says that He didn't give, he is lying; because He gave but he doesn't realize (what God is giving). (For example) Generosity gave him (the fact) that he wanted something that is not acceptable by his current reality. There no contraction at all!

[**Endurance and Permanence:**]

The endurance (*baqaa*) of this existent, just as all others (who may be described by endurance), is maintained by the enduring (*ibqaa"*) of Allah (i.e. by His will to make the Single Monad endured) not by His endurance (*baqaa"*), because the Possible is endured by the enduring of his preponderator, not by his endurance, otherwise: if his endurance was by the endurance of Allah, this means that he is with Him eternally, and if he was with Him eternally he would be necessarily-existent, and he wouldn't be possible, but he is possible in himself, so he has to be endured by the enduring of Allah (bot by His Endurance).

The condition of his endurance is the continuous provision from Allah, the Cherished and the Glorified, by keeping his existence on him and making him accepting the sciences and knowledge from Him.

The Preponderator, Who is the Exalted Creator, is not forced to offer this provision, but He has the choice (i.e. He is *mukhtaar*) to do whatever He wishes. But we knew that He willed the perpetual endurance (for the Single Monad), so His Wish doesn't change, because of His primordial knowledge, as, the Exalted, said: *there is no changing for the Words of Allah* [*Quran*: 10.64], and, the Exalted, said: *the sentence that comes from Me cannot be changed* [*Quran*: 50.29], and, the Exalted, said: *but the word of doom (for disbelievers) is fulfilled* [*Quran*: 39.71].

Otherwise, there is no way to know the endurance of the Intellect, and all other possibles that may be endured, until He tells us that. Such knowledge may not be achieved by proofs at all; whoever claims that he knew the endurance of the Possibles by the way of prove, he'd better review his proof, because it is a guess and not a proof!

Therefore, his endurance is by the preservation of Allah, the Exalted, and His (continuous) provision, just as the body is preserved by its form (that is continuously being re-created in ever new forms); if He holds the creation of the form it would cease to exist.

So we have shown his need of endurance, and his existence through the appearance of his essence, and his endurance according to the law (stated through the various Quranic verses quoted above).

It remained for us to show (in what follows) his perfection (and completeness).

[**His Perfection:**]

He is also perfect in himself. The meaning of his perfection is his (unconditional) ability to accept the emanations of his Creator, that He emanates on him in (continuous) sequence.

We know that if he was not always in such perfect readiness, he wouldn't be able to accept something, but he is never unable, because Allah made his creation perfect.

[**His Completeness:**]

And he is also described by completeness, because everything is (or exists) in him in effect, i.e. by (primordial) knowledge and (effective) force (even before the existence of their essences), since all things exist though him, and he is (always) ready to accept them. In fact, they are existing in him (at the time when their essences are brought into existence, so he is the essence of everything!).

[So He is Created:]

This indicates that he is created (*muhdath*); he was not and then he is, because he became a place to what Allah creates in him, which are the created things. So since he is always the place for them (i.e. those created things), since the time his essence existed, thus he is also created like them.

[The Length and Breadth of Spirits and Bodies:]

Then you should know that this existent (that is the Single Monad) is the one who gives the things according to the length and the width (or breadth).

The meaning of length in him is what he gives out to the spirits of what keeps their capability and continuity, and the meaning of width is what he gives to the bodies of what makes them survive, by (continuously) updating their states (or forms), just as knowledge is (continuously) updating on the spirits.

[His Length and Breadth are Equal:]

His length and breadth have equal facets. (This observation supports the astounding conclusion we have reached through the Duality of Time Theory, that the structure of the psychical world should exactly identical with the physical objects, with the same kinds of elementary particles, atoms, crystals, and even rocks and mountains. The only difference between the corporeal and incorporeal worlds is that they evolve in orthogonal time dimensions, and that's why they don't interact directly. In the Ultimate Symmetry, we showed how this critical issue can solve the problems of super-symmetry and matter-antimatter asymmetry, because that the fermions in our physical world behave as bosons in the psychical world, and vice versa. Therefore, the length and width of the Single Monad are the two identical folds of the missing super-symmetry. What is even more interesting is that Ibn al-Arabi specifies in the following that both the length and the width have 180,000 facets, making a total of 360,000. It is therefore obvious that this is the origin of the ancient Sumerian system of dividing the circle into 360 degrees and the heavens into 12 zodiac sighs. This Sexagesimal system is not a mere convention, and we could only make a note here that in complex analysis, of modern mathematics, it has been found, without any solid proof, that one over the sum of all integer numbers should be equal to 12!)

[**The Origin of the Sexagesimal System:**]

He has 180,000 facet in length, and 180,000 facet in width, and each facet has 24,000 form, and each form has numerous thins, no one knows their number except Allah, and each thin has many forces, no one knows them except Allah; and they ascending and descending.

Through these thins of this Intellect, Allah creates, in their ascending and descending, what happens in the world, both high and low, of everything. These are called the ascensions (*al-maarij*), as the Exalted, said: *a questioner questioned concerning the doom about to fall* [*Quran*: 70.1], and that's the descending (or *falling*), and so is the Mercy (is also falling on those who deserve it). Then He said: *(falling) upon the disbelievers. None can repel it* [*Quran*: 70.2], *from Allah*, because He is the One Who is creating things *next to* it, not through it (i.e. next to the causes, not through them.). Then He said: *Who has the ascensions* [*Quran*: 70.3], which are the thins (just mentioned above), *(whereby) the angels (and the Spirit) ascend* [*Quran*: 70.4], which are the spiritual forces that we have mentioned.

So look how wonderful is Quran to those whom Allah enlightened their sight, and made them (dedicated) for Himself.

[**The Cyclic Nature of Existence:**]

Since the matter (in this Lower World) is about ascending and descending, it is cyclical, with a circular shape like the wheel. And also in the Hereafter; its pleasure circulates in it just as in this world, with different and endless forms, no form is ever like the other, to everyone his pleasure (in the Gardens).

Also for the people of Fire, doom circulates according to their age, and then it returns on them multiplied.

That's why Allah said (about the people of Misery): *and it is given to them similar* [*Quran*: 2.25], and: *as often as their skins are consumed We shall exchange them for other skins* [*Quran*: 4.56].

And He said (for the people of Happiness): *and the end of their prayer is: Praise be to Allah, the Lord of the worlds* [*Quran*: 10.10], and then it returns to the beginning. So the beginning of prayer was "*there is no god but Allah*", and the end of it is "*praise be to Allah*", and between them are Magnification (*Allahu Akbar*), Glorification (*Subhaana Allah*), Praising (*al-hamdu li-Allah*) and other than that.

Likewise in everything, there are cycles and circles. In the human being, his knowledge of himself is his knowledge of his Lord; so it is circular, because whenever he knew a description of himself he knew a description of his Lord, then he descends back to himself with another knowledge from which he ascends with it to another knowledge of his Lord, according to what it indicates of the self-knowledge, then this Lord-knowledge brings him back down for what he has of the need to more increase

[The Cyclic Nature of Existence:]

(in knowledge), and so on.

That's why the Exalted said to His Prophet, may Allah have peace and mercy upon him: *and say: O my Lord, increase me in knowledge* [*Quran*: 20.114].

And also like that is knowledge of the Divine Presence; from its action to its descriptions to its essence,[15] then the circle returns in these three, but the tastes vary; whenever one thin of those thins (mentioned above) returns off from an existent, another thin takes over, and this thin moves to another existent, always circling like that.

For example, when you move in water, or air, whenever you move over to some place you leave another, and that which was occupying it moves to fill the place that you left.

Allah, the Exalted, said: *and We said: Smite him with some of it (i.e. the Cow that Allah ordered the people of Israel to slaughter so that they will know who is the killer, in the famous story.). Thus Allah brings the dead to*

---

[15] As we have seen in the previous volumes, Ibn al-Arabi always affirms that there are three types of divine names: Names of Essence (*Asmaa al-Dhaat*), the Names of Descriptions or the Attributes (*Asmaa al-Sifaat*) and the Names of Actions (*Asmaa al-Afaal*) [*Futuhat*: I.423.20, I.67.28].

life [*Quran*: 2.73], (so, the spirit of the slaughtered cow replaced that of the dead persons, thus he was able to speak and tell who has killed him!) so nothing may inhabit a place before it leaves another. Be pay attention to the (exchanging) roles of life and death. It is amazing, because it is happening in every breath ever (although we do not observe the difference between the ever-new forms, as Allah Said): *"and it is given to them similar"*.

Also, (the Prophet) may Allah have mercy and peace upon him, said: *"The spirits of the martyrs are in bird's gorges, hanged in the fruits of Paradise"* [*Kanz: 11107, 11127, 11169, 11170, 11171, 11740*], and the Exalted said (about martyrs): *Nay, they are living. With their Lord they have provision* [*Quran*: 3.169].

The body is a connected machine, and the soul is the one who feels happy and sad.

And the Exalted said with regards to them (i.e. the martyrs): (*And call not those who are slain in the way of Allah "dead."*) *Nay, they are living, only you don't feel* [*Quran*: 2.154], so He used the word of "feeling" to indicate that it is hidden. (This is compared to what we briefly mentioned above, and explained in the Ultimate Symmetry, that the incorporeal worlds have the same nature of our physical objects, except they are evolving in orthogonal dimensions of time, and that's why we don't normally interact with them. A closer example is also the world of dreams.)

From here we also deduce that the numerous senses the human, of the souls and other related forces, all return to one essence that is indivisible, but it is a single embodied monad that accept all these descriptions; so when it attracts it is called attractive and when it holds it is called holding, and likewise for all the rules that are for the human being, and maybe we shall mention that in details in another place, if Allah, the Exalted, wills.

[**The Emanation of the Intellect:**]

You should know that this First Intellect is alone what emanated from Allah, the Exalted.

The fact that emergence of things is in sequence is not a necessity implied by the Existence of the Real, and that, for example, there might emerge out of Him only one, and that it is impossible otherwise.

[The Choice of Creation:]

However, He wanted that, and wished it, and if He had wished that the world exists at all once, and nothing is dependent on anything, it would be not difficult for Allah (to do it like that). Also, if Allah had wished to create them in the hereafter without this (lower) world, so that each will take his state and his (destined) station without any previous commission, this wouldn't be difficult, for what we have said (at the beginning) that the Exalted is Willing and the world is possible. Therefore, what He created, i.e. the First Intellect, is one by the choice of the Praised and His previous Wish, and this may not be judged, i.e. that Allah created him alone, until that ruler (the Prophet) says that Allah created one.

[The Multiple Descriptions of the Intellect:]

Moreover, this created (Intellect), although he is one with respect to his essence, he still has (multiple) properties to be created with him, when he is created, such as his description whose essence is conditioned upon his existence, not as the whole.

Hence, He created not only one, but two, or three creations, for what Allah created in him of (other) descriptions.

If the ruler says that he is one real, this means that he is one stand-alone creation.

[The Choice of Allah, the Exalted:]

So let's return to the fact that Allah always have the choice.

Thus we say, according to what we have established, that there no meaning for "ability" other than its relation to all that is possible of itself, and the reality of the Possible doesn't allow it to decline its effect. When we saw that the reality of the Possible doesn't allow the declination (to be brought into existence) and that the ability relates (to the Possible) by itself, and we didn't see all the Possibles happening all at once, we then definitely knew that (the one) Who is described by the Ability, if He was not Free-to-choose and Willing and that He already knew the existence of this one (that is the Intellect) - not the existence of all at once - we wouldn't have imagined that (He created only one)!

We say: He is Willing, Free-to-choose, and He does whatever He wishes, as the Exalted said: *(He is the) Doer of what He wills* [*Quran*: 11.107, 85.16], and (He) said: *"And ye will not, unless Allah wills"* [*Quran*: 76.30, 81.29], and (He) said: *and if We had so willed, We could have given every soul its guidance, but the word from Me took effect* [*Quran*: 32.13], which is His previous (predestined) Wish and Knowledge; no doer in Existence other than Him.

[**The One-to-Many Relation:**]

Therefore, you should know that the meaning of the maxim of those who say: *"only one may emerge from the one"* should not be taken according to the dissidents of the people of truth; those whose insight is blind from seeing through by the light of the law, and the safe mind, because they are judging about the things that may not be known by other than the way of unveiling, or through the narration of the honest (such as the Prophet, or the Sage, who narrates) after Allah - not by

[The One-to-Many Relation:]

intellectual thinking.[16]

They are claiming in what they said that Allah is One from all aspects, i.e. He has no any description; so nothing may emerge out of Him other than what accords to His Oneness, that is one, and then they rendered that this one (that is the Intellect) is with Him eternally, so they negated that Allah is his creator.

Then they said: *"and this one that emerged out of Him is possible (existent) and is three with different aspects; that he realized himself, he realized his maker and he realized that he is possible"*.

However, what adds to the blindness of the their sight is that they forgot that this (ill logic) requires them (to say the same) for the case of the Absolute Being that He is (also) a realizing (*aql*: intellect), He realized that He is necessarily-existent, and He realized this dependent existent, and maybe if they

---

[16] The author here is obviously alluding to the Muatazilites who argue that Allah may not be described by any attributes, otherwise these attributes or descriptions would be existing with Him eternally, so this would lead to eternal multiplicity. Apparently, this deviated thinking, widely criticized by the mainstream Asharites, is inherited from various Greek philosophers, such as Plotinus.

search another fourth realization will be added that he realized that his creator is necessary - because if he realized his creator this doesn't lead to his realizing that He is necessary - and also it is not possible that he only realized himself that they said: *"and he realized that he is possible"*, so they proved a third state, then the fourth is equally required, and so also the creator realizes that he is possible so he will also have four (states). Therefore, four things will emerge from Him, one for each one, and all this is in fact endless long hallucination.

(The rest of this section is added by the translator:

This critical issue, of the relation between oneness and multiplicity, has been explained in several places in the Single Monad of the Cosmos book series. In this regard, Ibn al-Arabi quotes the Pole of Spirits, who is Prophet Idris, known in the Bible as Enoch, saying that "the world exists between the circumference and the point" [*Futuhat*: I.154.22]. The secret of geometry, and thus: physics and cosmology, is encoded in this statement, because it is the key to unravel the mystery of space and time.

This simple statement is demonstrated in

[The One-to-Many Relation:]

Figure 7 that illustrate the principal concept of the Single Monad Model.

Ibn al-Arabi then explained that the "abstract point" at the center of the circle meets "any point" in the circumference with its "whole entity", without division or multiplicity. Similarly, all the creations are emerging from the Real, without affecting His unique Oneness or Unicity. However, the problem is that physical entities are different from the above abstract mathematical example of the circle and its center point, depicted in Figure 7. Nevertheless, with the correct understanding of the real flow of time, according to the Single Monad Model and Duality of Time Theory, the ultimate purely-geometrical nature of creation is revealed in a unique manner that connects the multiplicity of creation with the ultimate Oneness and Unicity of the One and Unique God, Who is the Creator of all corporeal and incorporeal worlds, without being multiplied in Himself or composed of any other (sub)entities.

When we understand this essential issue of one-to-many relation, we will be able to solve many fundamental problems in philos-

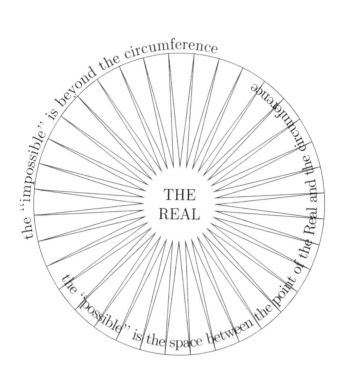

Figure 7: Despite their multiplicity, the indivisible central point, denoting the Real, meets each point from the circumference of the circle of creation. This One-to-Many relation can only be conceived with the oneness of time; that the individual entities of the multiplicity of creation may exist only one at a time, while the Single Monad is alternating between them.

ophy, physics, cosmology, and mathematics, because this is the key that connects between discreteness and continuity which are reflected on various levels in Nature, such as: space - time, wave - particle, energy - mass, singularities - infinities and many other less obvious dualities.

Ibn al-Arabi was well aware that this paradoxical relation between the Creator and all manifestations is in clear apparent contradiction with the widely accepted philosophical maxim, a central assumption in the prevailing contemporary Neo-Platonist philosophical cosmology, that "from the One only one can emerge (or proceed)". Logically, according to our normal simple intuition that is primarily based on physical embodiment, it is not possible to imagine a relation between the One and the many without affecting the unique Oneness of the One, because He must meet each individual one at the same time, so He must have many simultaneous aspects. Ibn al-Arabi solves this riddle by asserting that the interface between the One and all the many existent things doesn't happen all at once. Rather, at any single instance of time, there is in reality only one single relation or interface, a unique divine "with-ness", as he calls it, following the Quran [57:4], between the One and only "one" of the many multitudes of entities in the world. But what happens at this particular instance with the other entities, since their existence is preserved only through this unique creative relation between them and their Creator? The answer is: they do cease to exist, but their existence is maintained by (immediately) re-creating them again, perpetually. As we have repeated explained in the previous volumes, this principle of re-creation, or the "ever-renewed creation", is based on some central verses from Quran, including: (Are We tiered of the first creation? Nay, but they are unaware of the creation anew.) [50:15], and: (each Day He is upon one task) [55:29].

Therefore, in order to understand the relation between the unique Oneness of the Real and the apparent multiplicity of creations, Ibn al-Arabi adds time to the previous philosophical statement, which can be then restated as:

"from the One only one can proceed at

[The One-to-Many Relation:]

a time."

Ibn al-Arabi, however, affirms that this particular mode of creation was chosen by Allah to be like that, although in fact He might have created the world in any other way, so it is not any external restriction imposed over Him, the Exalted. In other words, this principle is not necessarily implied by the Existence of the Real, that only one can proceed from Him at a time, and that it is impossible otherwise. But He willed that, and if He had wished that the world should exist all at once, and that nothing were ever dependent on anything else, it wouldn't be difficult for Allah to create it like that. In such a case we would be living in a completely different logic. Yet, even within this primordial source of our current logic, causality is a macroscopic statistical phenomena and not any designated principle that cannot be broken. Therefore, because it explains the dynamic emergence of space-time geometry, the Duality of Time Theory explains the very cause of causality and how it can be broken in certain circumstances, such as the non-local behavior of quantum tunneling and entanglement.

The genuine complex-time explains how the geometry itself is being created dynamically, so the Universe becomes self-contained without any other predefined background geometry or topology. The dynamically created time-time geometry is essentially granular, but this depends on the relative position of the observer. In a simple statement, since observation is an instance of time, the observer exists in a fractal dimension between two consecutive complete integer spatial dimensions, as we are currently living, or evolving in the outward fractal dimension of time, between two and three spatial dimensions. Therefore, we will always "see" the two-dimensional space continuous, because we only see it after its creation, while the three-dimensional space will be discrete because we "see" it only one two-dimensional image at a time, but we can then "imagine" it to be continuous because we integrate these images with their supersymmetrical psychological folds to imagine the third dimension. In reality, however, this third dimension is only achieved as we progress with time and does not itself evolve in time, from our current position in this Lower World, though this might be the case in the Hereafter as we described in Chapter VII of the Single Monad Model.

Therefore, to correct this wrong induction that starts from the postulation that Allah has no essential descriptions or attributes, we need to define them correctly in the following. The author also explained this critical issue in the Book of Eternity, that's volume II in this series.)

[**The Types of Descriptions:**]

You should know that descriptions are two kinds: descriptions of essence and descriptions of meaning.

The descriptions of essence are that which the essence is not conceived without them, because they are (the essence) itself, nothing additional.

And the descriptions of meaning are those which the essence is conceived without them.

Knowing the essence of a thing leads to knowing its self-descriptions (or the descriptions of essence), but knowing these descriptions from the aspect of its being as such gives another meaning.

Please understand this (critical difference)!

This another description that is known to the essence, from the aspect of its being as such, necessitates a judgment on the essence. For example, when "knowledge" is attributed to the essence, so that it is (described as) knowing.

It is utterly known for granted that knowledge, for everyone with a safe mind, is one of the meanings, and the meaning doesn't stand alone.

Therefore, if the Essence of the Creator, the Exalted, is described by knowledge then this would be a meaning that will require an essence to stand. If knowledge (itself) was the Essence of the Creator, then knowledge would be a stand-alone (essence), which contradicts the reality of knowledge (that it is an abstract meaning).

We already showed that this whose essence is one doesn't multiply for what stands in it of meanings, no matter how many. The rule of the essence in things is due its being (described by) something, not due to itself, and this meaning that it necessitates is one, so it necessitates nothing but one.

[How Multiplicity is Emerging:]

Thus we say that the Praised Creator, from His being Willing when He is creating, and "creation" is one reality, though it is ascribed to the existing things that are many. Therefore, nothing is emerging from Him, from His being Willing, but the endowing of the Possible with one of the two possibilities, though the endowed (things) are many. Likewise, nothing is emerging from His being Knowing of this possible other than His regulating, though the regulated (things) are many.

Therefore, since the Ability is one, it gave only one reality, and that is creating the Possible. And Willing is one, and it gave the endowing of the Possible with one of the two possibilities, and endowing is but one meaning, and creating is also one meaning. And so every possible, when it is created, is created by the Ability, endowed with Willing and regulated by Knowledge; so nothing emerged out of the One except one (reality).

hence, if one of the essences of these possibles is created, and not many of them are created, this is by the rule of His Wish, the

Praised, just as if many of them were created, then it would be (also) by the rule of His Wish, the Praised.

This is the correct meaning of the saying that *"from the one nothing might emerge except one"*: if we see a possible thing has happened, we say its creation is a result of this, and its endowing is a result of that, and so on (every property is a result of one attribute of the Essence of the Creator, and the attributes, or descriptions of the Essence, - no matter how many - do not multiply the Essence.).

[**The Effect of Ability:**]

We also showed that the essence is not multiplied for the meanings that stand in it, because the description is not part of the described.

Also, it is impossible for anything in existence, other than Allah, the Exalted, to have any ability or a force - I mean independently - to create an essence or bring out something into existence. This is because its relation to the possible things is for themselves (not something that can be chosen or selected). Therefore, no predestined may ever resist it.

[The Effect of Ability:]

Therefore, the ability of the existing things doesn't have any effect by itself, but only with the permission of Allah, the Exalted. The old Ability, that is to Allah, the Exalted, is what creates the actions of the creations, high and low - when their will is directed and their ability is related with them (i.e. with the intended actions). Hence, there is (indeed) no doer but He.

That's why it cannot be imagined that someone may conceive of relating the ability to the destined things, because the created ability doesn't have any effect on the things independently.

By this description the clear difference is set between the Creator and the creation. However, no one may witness this scene, that is one of the divine characteristics. This is what is meant by His saying, the Exalted: *I made them not to witness the creation of the Heavens and the Earth, nor their own creation* [*Quran*: 18.51].

I take refuge with Allah (to think otherwise, that anyone else can do anything independently of Him.)! I do not share with Him anyone!

[**The Concurrence of Causes and Results:**]

(Here comes the most important conclusion of the Single Monad Model of the Cosmos: that what usually observe as causes and results are utterly unrelated, since nothing in reality has any intrinsic ability to do anything! the fact of the matter is that both the causes and the results are created by Allah, nothing else. Therefore, the apparent causal relations have no genuine reality, except that they are happening concurrently. Allah is creating the results next to the causes and not through them. This critical conclusion, that is a consequence of the Re-creation Principle of the Single Monad Model, solves many fundamental problems in modern physics and provide a logical interpretation to the weird quantum behavior, as we explained in the Duality of Time Theory and Ultimate Symmetry. Thus, Ibn al-Arabi concludes that:)

These causes, that you see actions happening next to them, are not like what the weak-minded think, but Allah, the Exalted, made them causes by creating the results next to them (*indaha*, and through them: *biha*).

[The Concurrence of Causes and Results:] 99

The causes are not making any actions, and also the Praised is not creating the actions through them, otherwise He would be needing them. Anything that leads to such needfulness by Him is impossible. It is not possible that He is in need.

The fact of the matter is that He is creating (the actions) next to them in order to deviate whoever He wishes and guide whoever He wishes, and to exhibit His (predestined) care of some people and His abandoning others (by letting their weak minds to deceive them.).

It is not as some weak-minded say that the motion of the hand is the motion of the sleeve, and the motion of the finger is the motion of the ring.

If they could realize and were enlightened by the light of the intellect, they would discover that the body, and everything that moves, doesn't move in occupied space (*malaa*) but in vacuum (*khalaa*), so this body, or the moving thing, that they claim it is moving by the motion of that mover (i.e. the cause) into a new place, may not move into this place before it is evacuated from what is occupying it, according to them. Look how easy this issue is, and how much veiled is the one who disagrees. Allah (alone) is able to do everything.

[**The Apparent Order of the World:**]

Therefore, after what we said, if we - or someone else (of the scholars) - talked about the arrangement of the order of the World and the dependence of some of it parts on others, we only talk about it as Allah arranged it, not that this is how its reality requires, and that no other way is possible.

In fact, this arrangement is possible just like any other. (For example) Allah may create the world of bodies before the world of spirits. (Not) As some (other opinions) who oppose the people of truth and say that the partial souls must have been after the creation of bodies, and the Possible may never be necessary for itself, and the necessity of a thing is only comprehended for itself. According to the law, necessity doesn't revoke the Possible from the reality of its possibility. If it was true that the Possible may become necessary, and that this is required by the mind, then it will also require that the necessary will also become possible, and this leads to falsifying the realities. Then no (logical) knowledge will be in our hands at all.

Therefore, the Possible has to remain possible, and the necessary necessary - because He is necessary by Himself - and the Impossible impossible, because it is impossible for itself.

[Conclusion:]

This is what Allah caused it to flow in this tight time in answering this issue, and we have simplified and repeated the words on it for the sake of the understanding of those who shall be studying it, since not all understandings are sharp enough to understand the summarized words.

May Allah the Praised make us benefit by knowledge, and make us amongst His people, by His grace, no Lord but Him.

The answer is complete, and praise is to Allah the Giver, the Generous and the Charitable.

May Allah have peace and mercy upon our master Muhammad, the unlettered Prophet, and on his family and friends.

Books by Mohamed Haj Yousef

Mohamed Haj Yousef is a writer and researcher interested in physics, cosmology, philosophy and Islamic thought, especially with regard to mysticism and Ibn al-Arabi.

He published numerous articles in Arabic and English that combine science, philosophy and Islamic thought. Most of these articles are accessible online at: ibnalarabi.com.

He also published several books on the subject of time, and other related subjects in Islamic thought and Sufi mysticism, including:

The Sufi Interpretation of Joseph Story: (The Path

of the Heart from Existence to Perishing and the to Endurance), al-Marifa (Aleppo, Beirut), CreateSpace (Charleston), Paperback: 410 pages, ISBN: 978-1482022445, 1482022443, First Published: 1999

The Sun from the West: Biography of Ibn al-Arabi and His Doctrine, First Published in 2006 by Dar Fussilat (Aleppo), Second Edition: 2013, CreateSpace (Charleston), Paperback: 708 pages, ISBN: 978-1482020229, 148202022X

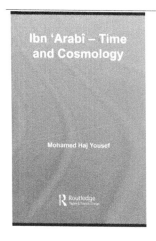

Ibn Arabi - Time and Cosmology, Routledge (New York, London), hardback/Paperback: 256 pages, ISBNs:, (paperback) 978-0415664011/0415664012, (hardback) 978-0415444996/0415444993, (electronic) 978-0203938249, First Published: 2007

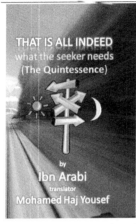

That Is All Indeed: what the seeker needs, CreateSpace (Charleston), Paperback: 74 pages, ISBN: 978-1482077421, 1482077426, First Published: 2010

The Meccan Revelations: (introduction), Amazon - kindle, Paperback: 180 pages, ASIN: B00B0G1S5Y
First Published: 2012

The Meccan Revelations: (volume 1 of 37), By Muhyiddin Ibn Arabi, Trns. by: Mohamed Haj Yousef
Publisher: CreateSpace (Charleston), Paperback: 400 pages, ISBN: 978-1549641893, 1549641891, First Published: 2012

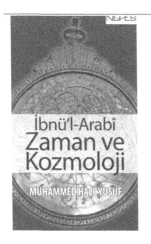

Ibnu'l-Arabi Zaman ve Kozmoloji, By Mohamed Haj Yousef, (Turkish translation of: Ibn Arabi-Time and Cosmology), Trns. by: Kadir Filiz, Nefes Yayincilik (Istanbul), Paperback: 256 pages, ISBN: 978-6055902377, 6055902370, First Published: 2013

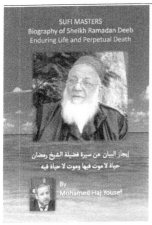

Biography of Sheikh Ramadan Deeb, Tayba-al-Garraa (Damascus), CreateSpace (Charleston), Paperback: 400 pages, ISBN: 978-1482014419, 1482014416, First Published: 2013

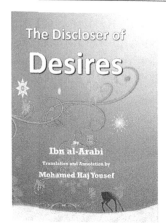

The Discloser of Desires, (turjuman al-ashwaq), By Muhyiddin Ibn Arabi, Trns. by: Mohamed Haj Yousef, CreateSpace (Charleston), Paperback: 200 pages, ISBN: 978-1499769678, 1499769679, First Published: 2014

The Days of God, By Mohamed Haj Yousef, (Arabic translation of the Single Monad Model of the Cosmos), CreateSpace (Charleston), Paperback: 488 pages, ISBN: 978-1482022919, 1482022915, First Published: 2014

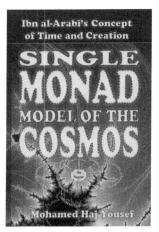

The Single Monad Model of the Cosmos, CreateSpace (Charleston), Paperback: 352 pages, ISBN: 978-1499779844, 1499779844, First Published: 2014

DUALITY OF TIME: Complex-Time Geometry and Perpetual Creation of Space, (this book), CreateSpace (Charleston), Paperback: 360 pages, ISBN: 978-1539579205, 1539579204, First Published: 2018

ULTIMATE SYMMETRY: Fractal Complex-Time, Quantum Gravity and the Incorporeal World, Independently published, Paperback: 323 pages, ISBN: 978-1723828690, 1723828696, First Published: Jan. 2019

TIME CHEST: Particle-Wave Duality from Time Confinement to Space Transcendence, Independently published, Paperback: 220 pages, ISBN: 978-1793927156

Bibliography

Yahya, U. (1964). *Histoire et classification de l'oeuvre d'Ibn 'Arabi.* Institut Français de Damas.

Yousef, M. (2006). *The Sun from the West: Biography of the Greatest Master Muhyiddin Ibn al-Arabi and His Doctrine.* Dar Fussilat, Aleppo.

Yousef, M. (2013). *The Sun from the West: Biography of Ibn Arabi and His Doctrine.* CreateSpace Independent Publishing Platform.

Yousef, M. (2019). *The Sun from the West: Biography of the Greatest Master Muhyiddin Ibn al-Arabi and His Doctrine.* Independently Published.

[الخاتمة]

فهذا بعض ما أجرى الله تعالى في الوقت، على ضيقه، من الجواب في هذه المسألة، وبسطنا القول فيها وكررنا من أجل فهم الناظر فيها، فإنه ليس كل فهم يكون له سرعة النفوذ، وفهم الكلام الموجز، والله سبحانه ينفعنا بالعلم، ويجعلنا من أهله بمنّهِ لا رب غيره.

تم الجواب، والحمد لله الوهاب، الجواد المحسان، وصلى الله على سيدنا محمد النبي الأمي وعلى آله وصحبه وسلم.

هذا أنه يُحرِّك بحركته هذا المتحرك إلى حيِّزه، أنّه لا يتحرَّك إلى حيِّز المتحرِّك المتولّد عنه حتى يفرغ هذا المحل، على زعمه، أحيازه التي هو فيها (فتكون النتيجة سابقة للفعل!)؛ فانظر ما أقرب وجه المسألة، وما أعمى المخالف عنها! والله على كل شيء قدير.

[سبب ترتيب نضد العالم]

فإذا تقرر ما ذكرناه وتكلم أحد، أو تكلمنا، على ترتيب نضد العالم، وتوقف بعضه على بعض؛ فإنما نتكلم عليه على حسب ما رتبه الله، لا على أن ذلك تقتضيه حقيقته، وأنه لا يجوز إلا ذلك، بل يمكن هذا الترتيب، ويمكن خلافه، ويمكن أن يوجد الله عالَم الأجسام قبل عالَم الأرواح، (لا) كما يقول بعض مخالفي أهل الحق أن النفوس الجزئية متأخرة عن وجود الأجسام، والممكن لا يصير واجباً أبداً لذاته، ولا يُعقل وجوب شيء إلا لذاته، والوجوب الشرعي لا يزيل الممكن عن حقيقة إمكانهُ ولو صح أن يصير الممكن واجباً يقتضيه العقل لاقتضى أيضاً أن يصير الواجب ممكناً، وأدى ذلك إلى بطلان الحقائق، ولم يبق بأيدينا علم أصلاً!

فلا بد أن يبقى الممكن ممكناً، لأنه لنفسه هو ممكن، والواجب واجباً، لأنه لنفسه هو واجب، والمحال محالاً، لأنه لنفسه هو محال.

قدرتهم بها، فلا فاعل إلا هو.

ولهذا لا يُتصوَّرُ أن يعقل أحد تعلُّق القدرة بالمقدور، لكون القدرة الحادثة ليس لها تأثير في الأشياء بالاستقلال، وبهذه الصفة يقع الفرق الجلي بين الخالق والمخلوق، وهذا المشهد لا يشهده أحد أبداً، وهو من الخصائص الإلهية، وهو قوله تعالى: (مَّا أَشْهَدتُّهُمْ خَلْقَ السَّمَاوَاتِ وَالْأَرْضِ وَلَا خَلْقَ أَنفُسِهِمْ) [18: 51]، ونعوذ بالله، لا أشرك به أحداً!

[السببية العِنديّة]

وهذه الأسباب، التي ترى وقوع الفعل عندها، ليس كما يتخيله الضعيف العقل، ولكن الله تعالى جعلها أسباباً بفعل المسبَّبات "عندها"، لا هي تفعلها، ولا هو سبحانه يفعله بها، ولو كان ذلك لكان مضطراً إليها، وكل ما يؤدي إلى افتقار منه يستحيل عليه الافتقار فهو محال؛ ولكن (الله سبحانه هو الذي) يفعله "عندها" (لا: بها، ولا: هي تفعله بنفسها، وذلك الوهمُ) ليُضلَّ (اللهُ به) من يشاء ويَهدي من يشاء، وليظهر عنايته لقوم، وخذلانه لقوم آخرين.

لا كما يقول بعض الضعفة العقل: إن حركة اليد (هي) حركة الكُمّ، وحركة الأصبع (هي) حركة الخاتم! ولو علم واستنار بنور العقل، أنَّ الجسم، وكلَّ ما يتحرك، أنه لا يتحرك في الملاء، وإنما يتحرك في الخلاء، فلا بدَّ أن يكون الجسم أو المتحرك الذي يدَّعي

عنه من كونه عالماً بهذا الممكن إلا إحكامه، والمحكومون كثيرون، فإذاً: فالقدرة واحدة، فأعطت حقيقة واحدة، وهو إيجاد الممكن، والإرادة واحدة وأعطت حقيقة اختصاص الممكن بأحد الجائزين، والاختصاص معنى واحد، والإيجاد معنى واحد، وكل ممكن إذا وُجد فهو موجود بالقدرة، مختص بالإرادة، محكم بالعلم، فما صدر عن الواحد إلا واحد.

فإن وجد واحد من هذه الأعيان الممكنات، ولم يوجد منها كثيرون، فمن حكم مشيئته سبحانه، (تماماً، ولا فرق) كما لو وجد منها كثيرون، (وهذا) هو الذي يصح منه قول من يقول: لا يصدر عن الواحد إلا واحداً.

[تأثير القدرة]

فإذا رأينا ممكناً قد وقع، قلنا وجوده عن كذا، واختصاصه عن كذا، وقد بيَّنا أنَّ الذات لا تتعدد بما يقوم بها من المعاني، فإن الصفة ليست بجزء الموصوف، ومن المحال أن يكون لموجود في الوجود من الموجودات قدرة، أو قوة، أي بالاستقلال، على إيجاد عين، وإبراز موجود، إلا الله تعالى (فهو وحده القادر على ذلك)، فإن تعلقها (أي تعلق القدرة) بالممكنات، لذاتها، فلا يخرج عنها مقدور البتة (أي يخرج عن حكمها).

وإن القدرة التي للموجودات لا تأثير لها، أي بذاتها، إلا بإذن الله تعالى، وإن القدرة القديمة، التي هي لله تعالى، هي التي توجد أفعال الخلق، أعلاه وأسفله، عند توجه إرادتهم، وتعلق

نفسها، ليست شيئا زائداً. وصفات المعنى هي التي تعقل الذات ولا هي.

والعلم بذات الشيء يعطي معرفة صفاته النفسية، ومعرفة تلك الذات من كونها كذا يعطي معنى آخر، فاعلم ذلك.

وذلك الأمر الآخر، المعلوم للذات من كونها كذا، يوجب حكماً للذات، فيحكم على الذات (مثلاً): إذا قام بها "علم" أنها "عالمة".

ومعلوم قطعاً أن العلم، عند كل ذي عقل سليم، معنى من المعاني، والمعنى لا يقوم بنفسه.

فلو كانت ذات الباري تعالى هي العلم، لكانت معنى، ولطلبت ما يقوم به، ولو كان العلم ذات الباري، لكان العلم قائماً بنفسه، وهذا يناقض حقيقة العلم.

وقد بيَّنَّا (في أوّل هذا الكتاب) أنَّ الأحدي الذات لا يتكثّر بما يقوم به من المعاني، بالغة ما بلغت، والحكم للذات في الأشياء إنما هو لكونها كذا، لا لنفسها، وذلك المعنى الذي يوجب، وهو واحد، فلا يوجب إلا واحداً.

[كيف تصدر الكثرة]

فنقول إن الباري، سبحانه، من كونه مريداً عند الإيجاد، والإيجاد حقيقة واحدة، وإن رجعت إلى نفس الموجودين، والموجودون كثيرون، ولا يصدر عنه من كونه مريداً إلا اختصاص الممكن بأحد الجائزين، لا غير، ويكون المخصوصون كثيرون، ولا يصدر

فيما قالوه: إن الله واحد من كل وجه، أي: ليس له صفة البتة، فلا يصدر عنه إلا ما تعطيه الوحدانية، وهو واحد، ثم جعلوا ذلك الواحدَ معه أزلاً، ونفوا أن يكون الله خالقاً له! ثم قالوا: وذلك الواحد الذي صدر عنه، هو ممكن، وهو ثلاثة باعتبارات مختلفة، وذلك أنه "عقل نفسه" و"عقل صانعه" و"عقل أنه ممكن"!

ومن عَمِي بصائرهم أنهم ما تفطنوا أن هذا يلزمهم (نفس الاستقراء) في حق الوجود المطلق، وهو إنه "عقل نفسه" و"عقل أنه واجب الوجود" و"عقل هذا للموجود المقيد"، وربما، إن بحثوا، يزيد لهم عقل رابع، وهو أنه عَقَل (كون) صانعه واجب، لأنه لا يلزم إذا عقل (كون) صانعه أنه ممكن، فأثبتوا مرتبة ثالثة، فيلزمهم الرابعة، لزوماً صحيحاً، ويكون الباري أيضاً يَعقل هذا ممكّناً، فتكون أيضاً أربعة، فتوجد عنه أربعة أشياء: لكل واحد واحد، وهذا هذيان طويل لا تحصيل له.

(ولتصحيح هذا الاستقراء، الذي يبدأ من القول بأن الله سبحانه وتعالى واحد ليس له صفة، لا بدَّ من تحقيق معنى الصفات وكيفية نسبتها إلى الله، وهو ما سيقوم به الشيخ في بقية هذا الكتاب، كما أنَّه فصَّل ذلك أيضاً في كتاب الأزل، وفي مواضع كثيرة في الفتوحات المكية.)

[الصفات على نوعين]

فاعلم أنا نقول إن الصفات على نوعين: صفات ذات، وصفات معنى. فصفات الذات هي التي لا تعقل الذات إلا بها، لأنها

[إن الله تعالى مختار]

فلنرجع لكونه تعالى مختاراً، ونقول، على حد ما قررناه، أنه: لا معنى للقدرة إلا تعلُّقها بكلِّ ممكنٍ، لذاتها، وليس في حقيقة الممكن أن يمتنع بنفسه عنها. فلما رأينا أن الممكن ليس من حقيقته الامتناع، ورأينا القدرة تتعلق لذاتها، ولم نر الممكنات وقعت بأسرها واحدة، علمناه على القطع أن الموصوف بالقدرة لو لم يكن مختاراً مريداً قد سبق في علمه وجود ذلك الواحد، لا وجود الكل دفعة واحدة، لما تُصوِّر هذا، فقلناه أنه: مريد، مختار، يفعل ما شاء، كما قال تعالى: (فَعَّالٌ لِمَا يُرِيدُ) [58: 16]، وقال: (وَمَا تَشَاءُونَ إِلَّا أَنْ يَشَاءَ اللَّهُ) [81: 29]، وقال: (وَلَوْ شِئْنَا لَآتَيْنَا كُلَّ نَفْسٍ هُدَاهَا وَلَكِنْ حَقَّ الْقَوْلُ مِنِّي) [32: 13]، وهو سبق المشيئة والعلم. لا فاعل في الوجود إلا هو.

[نظرية الفيض]

ثم اعلم أن معنى قول من قال: "إن الواحد لا يصدر منه إلا واحد"، فليس كما تخيله مخالفو أهل الحق، المطموسة بصائرهم عن الاستبصار بنور الشرع، والعقل السليم، حيث تحكموا في معرفة موجودات لا يصح إدراكها إلا بطريق الكشف، أو إخبار (النبيّ) الصادق، عن الله، لا غير. لا بالفكر، كما زعموا

الحق (تعالى)، وأنه مثلاً لا يمكن أن يصدر عنه إلا واحد، وأنَّ هذا محالٌ (أن يصدر عنه أكثر من واحد)، ولكن أراد ذلك، وشاءه، ولو شاء أن يوجد العالم كله دفعة واحدة ولا يترتب شيء على شيء، لما كان ذلك على الله بعزيز، ولو شاء الله أن يخلقهم في الأخرة دون الدنيا، ويُنزل كلَّ منزول منزله ومسكنه، من غير تكليف سابق، لم يكن ذلك عليه بعزيز؛ لما ذكرناه (في أوَّل هذا الكتّاب) من كونه تعالى مريداً، وكون العالم ممكناً.

فإنَّ (الله تعالى) ما أوجده، يعني العقل الأول، واحداً (إلا) اختياراً منه سبحانه وبسابق مشيئته، ولا يحكم بذلك، أي بكونه خلقه الله وحده، إلا حتى يقول الشارع (أي المُشرِّع) إنَّ الله خلق واحداً. حينئذ فهذا المخلوق، وإن كان واحداً من حيث ذاتُه، إلا أنه لا بدَّ أن يخلق معه في حال خلقه: "صفته"، التي هي مشروطة بوجوده، في عينها، لا من الجملة. فاذاً، فلم يخلق واحداً، وإنما خلق خلقين، أو ثلاثة؛ بما خلقه الله عليه من الصفات، فإذا جاء الشارع بأنه خلق واحداً، فمعناه أنَّه خلق واحداً قائماً بنفسه. (وفي ذلك إشارة إلى حديث النبي صلى الله عليه وسلم: "أول ما خلق الله العقل"، وفي حديث: "أول ما خلق الله نور نبيك يا جابر"، وفي حديث: "ثم خلق منه كلَّ خير")

دائمًا: (وَأُتُوا بِهِ مُتَشَابِهًا) [2: 25].[10]

وقد قال صلى الله عليه وسلم: «أرواح الشهداء في حواصل طير تعلق من ثمار الجنة»، وقال تعالى (عن الشهداء): (بَلْ أَحْيَاءٌ عِنْدَ رَبِّهِمْ يُرْزَقُونَ) [3: 169].

والجسم آلة موصولة، والنفس تفرح وتحزن، وقال تعالى فيهم: (وَلَا تَقُولُوا لِمَنْ يُقْتَلُ فِي سَبِيلِ اللَّهِ] أَمْوَاتٌ بَلْ أَحْيَاءٌ وَلَكِنْ لَا تَشْعُرُونَ) [2: 154]، فجاء بلفظ "الشعور" تنبيهًا على أن الأمر خفي، ومن هنا تعرف أنَّ العَدَد الذي يُرى في الإنسان: في النفوس (من تعدد الحواس) والقوى، وشبه ذلك، إنما يرجع ذلك (كلّه) إلى عين واحدة، لا تنقسم، بل هي جوهرٌ فردٌ متميزٌ، قابلٌ لهذه الأوصاف، فإذا جذبت سُمِّيت "جاذبة"، وإذا أمسكت سميت "ماسكة"، وهذا في جميع الأحكام التي للإنسان، وربما سنذكر ذلك إن شاء الله تعالى في موضوع آخر مستوفى.

[صدور العقل من الله تعالى]

واعلم أن هذا العقل الأول الصادر من الله تعالى وحده، وصدور الأشياء على التوالي ما (بمعنى ليس) ذلك لما يقتضيه وجود

---

[10] هذه الجملة الأخيرة مع الآية غير موجودة في المخطوطات، وهي من طبعة القاهرة، لكنَّ معناها صحيح ودقيق لكونها تشير إلى أن الأمر واقع في تجدد الخلق مع الأنفاس.

أهل الجنة، وقال في أهل النار: (كُلَّمَا نَضِجَتْ جُلُودُهُمْ بَدَّلْنَاهُمْ جُلُودًا غَيْرَهَا) [4: 56]، وقال: (وَآخِرُ دَعْوَاهُمْ أَنِ الْحَمْدُ لِلَّهِ رَبِّ الْعَالَمِينَ) [10: 10]، ويرجع (بعدها) إلى الأول، فأول الدعوى: "لا إله إلا الله"، وآخرها: "الحمد لله"، وما بينهما "تكبير" و"تسبيح" و"تحميد"، وغير ذلك.

وهكذا في كل شيء: أدوار، وأكوار.

ومعرفة الإنسان بنفسه مع معرفته بربه دورياً، فإنه كلما عرف صفة من نفسه عرف معرفة من ربه، ثم نزل إلى نفسه إلى معرفة أخرى منه، يصعد بها إلى معرفة أخرى من ربه، مما تدل عليه تلك المعرفة النفسية، ثم تنزل تلك المعرفة الربانية بما عنده من الافتقار إلى الزيادة، وهكذا (إلى ما لا نهاية له).

ولذلك قال تعالى لنبيه صلى الله عليه وسلم: (وَقُل رَّبِّ زِدْنِي عِلْمًا) [20: 114]، وهكذا المعرفة بالحضرة الإلهية: من "فعلها" إلى "صفتها" إلى "ذاتها"، ثم يدور الدور في هذه الثلاثة، وتتنوع المشارب، فهما انعطفت رقيقة من تلك الرقائق عن موجود، تلقته رقيقة أخرى، وانتقلت تلك الرقيقة إلى موجود آخر، دائرة هكذا، كما تمشي في الماء والهواء؛ إذا اختليت موضعاً، أخليت موضعاً آخراً لك، وانتقل عامره إلى موضعك الذي كنت فيه تعمره. قال الله تعالى: (فَقُلْنَا اضْرِبُوهُ بِبَعْضِهَا كَذَلِكَ يُحْيِي اللَّهُ الْمَوْتَى) [2: 73] (ومحط الشاهد أنَّ موت البقرة كان سبباً لازماً لإحياء المقتول) فما عمر شيء محلا إلا أخلي غيره، فتفطن لدور الحياة والموت، فإنه عجيب، أي لأنه واقع في كل نَفَسٍ

٤٠

[معنى المعارج]

وهذه التي تسمى "المعارج"، قال الله تعالى: (سَأَلَ سَائِلٌ بِعَذَابٍ وَاقِعٍ) [70: 1]، فانظر في قوله "واقع"، وهو النزول، وكذا الرحمة (أيضاً واقعة)، ثم قال: (لِلْكَافِرِينَ لَيْسَ لَهُ دَافِعٌ [2] مِنَ اللَّهِ) لكونه هو الخالق عندها، لا بها، ثم قال: (ذِي الْمَعَارِجِ [3])، وهي الرقائق، (تَعْرُجُ الْمَلَائِكَةُ)، وهي القوى الروحانية التي ذكرناها، (وَالرُّوحُ إِلَيْهِ)، وهو الموجود الأول، الذي ذكرناه (وهو هذا العقل الأول الذي نحن في حضرته).

فما أعجب القرآن لمن نور الله بصيرته، واصطنعه لنفسه.

[دورية الوجود]

ولما كان الأمر صعودا ونزولا كان الأمر دوريا كرّيَّ الشكل، مثل الدولاب، وكذلك الأخرة يدور نعيمها فيها على مقدار الدنيا (أي هي كذلك تحت حكم درجات العقل المذكرة آنفاً، ذات الطول والعرض، ومجموعها ثلاثمائة وستون درجة، حصرتها الأبراج الاثني عشر، ولكن) بصور مختلفة غير متناهية لا تشبه صورة أختها أبداً، يدور على كل إنسان نعيمه، أو عذابه في أهل النار، على قدر عمرهم، وينعطف عليهم متضاعفاً.

ولهذا قال تعالى: (وَأُتُوا بِهِ مُتَشَابِهًا) [2: 25]، (فيما يخص

وجدت عينه، وما لا يخلو عن الحوادث فهو حادث مثلها.

[الطول والعرض، للأرواح والأجسام]

ثم اعلم أن هذا الموجود (الذي هو العقل الأول) هو الذي يعطي الأشياء على "الطول" و"العرض".

ومعنى "الطول" فيه ما يعطي للأرواح مما به صلاحها وبقاؤها، ومعنى "العرض" فيه ما يعطي للأجسام مما به بقاؤها مع تنوع الحالات عليها، كما تتنوع المعارف على الأرواح (كذلك تتنوع الحالات على الأجسام).

[تساوي الطول والعرض]

وطوله وعرضه على التساوي في الوجوه.

[أصل درجات الدائرة]

فإنَّ له مائة ألف وثمانين ألف وجه في عرضه، لكل وجه أربعة وعشرون ألف صورة، مع كل صورة رقائق لا يعلم عددها إلا الله، لكل رقيقة قوىً لا يعلمها إلا الله، صاعدة ونازلة.

في تلك الرقائق من هذا العقل يخلق الله عند نزولها وعد صعودها ما يحدث في العالم أسفله وأعلاه من كل شيء.

عينه، وثبت له "البقاء" بالشرع، فبقي لنا "التمام" (أن نثبته فيما يلي).

[العقل الأول تام]

فهو أيضا "تام في نفسه"، ومعنى أنه تام (هو) قبوله لفيض موجده عليه ما يفيضه على التوالي من غير أن يعجز عن قبول شيء مما يفيضه عليه. فقد علمنا أنه لو لم يكن له استعداد تام لعجز عن قبول أمر ما، ولا يعجز، فالله قد أتم خلقه.

[العقل الأول كامل]

وله أيضا "الكمال" من حيث أن كل شيء (موجود) فيه بالفعل، أي (ب)العلم والقوة (يعني قبل وجوده بالعين)، فجميع الأشياء موجودة فيه، لأنه مستعد لقبولها، بل هي فيه (بالعين، لأنه هو الذي يظهرها).10

[العقل الأول مُحدَث]

هذا مما يدلك على أنه "مُحدث"، لم يكن ثم كان، لأنه قد صار محلا لما يخلق الله فيه، وهي الحوادث، وهو لم يخلُ عنها منذ

---
10 هذه العبارة غير واضحة في المخطوطات، وقد تم هنا إعادة صياغتها وتوضيحها.

[البقاء والإبقاء]

ولهذا الموجود (الذي هو العقل الأول)، وغيره، البقاء، بإبقاء الله، لا ببقائه (والضمير هنا عائد على "الله" تعالى)، أي: بقاء العقل محقق بإبقاء الله عليه الوجود، وليس ببقاء الله)، فإنَّ الممكن باقٍ، بإبقاءٍ مرجِّحه، لا ببقائه (أي "لا ببقاء مرجِّحه")، لأنه لو كان بقاؤه ببقاء الله لزم أن يكون معه أزلا، ولو كان معه أزلا لكان واجب الوجود، ولم يكن ممكنًا، وهو ممكن في نفسه، فلا بدَّ أن يكون باقيا بإبقاء الله. وعلة بقائه هو إمداد الله عزَّ وجلَّ أبداً بحفظ وجوده عليه، وتلقِّي العلوم والمعارف منه، والمرجِّح، وهو الباري تعالى، ليس بمجبور على الإمداد، وإنما هو مختار يفعل ما يشاء، فإن علمنا إنه قد شاء الإبقاء أبداً، فإنَّ مشيئته لا تتبدل، لسابق العلم، كما قال تعالى: (لَا تَبْدِيلَ لِكَلِمَاتِ اللَّهِ) [10: 64]، وقال تعالى: (مَا يُبَدَّلُ الْقَوْلُ لَدَيَّ) [50: 29]، وقال تعالى: (أَفَمَنْ حَقَّ عَلَيْهِ كَلِمَةُ الْعَذَابِ) [39: 19].

فلا سبيل إلى معرفة بقاء هذا العقل وجميع الممكنات التي يجوز بقاؤها إلا حتى يعرفنا بذلك ولا يوصل إلى معرفة ذلك بالبرهان، فإنه شبهة وليس ببرهان.

فإذا كان الأمر على ذلك، فكان بقاؤه بحفظ الله تعالى وإمداده، كما يبقي الجسم بعَرَضِه، فلو أمسك عنه خلق العرض، لعُدِم.[9]

فقد ثبت افتقاره إلى البقاء، وقد ثبت له الوجود بظهوره في

---

[9] هذا الفهم العميق متناسب مع ميكانيك الكمّ ...

[الوجود المحدث]

وهذا الموجود، الذي هو العقل، المقيد وجوده بالعدم، الموقوف على حكم المشيئة، الذي لم يكن ثم كان؛ لم يزل منذ وُجدت عينه يقبل الفيض الإلهي والجود المرسل بلطائف الغيب.

[الفيض لا ينقطع]

فإنَّ فيض الله تعالى لا يُتصور فيه مسك ولا قبض ولا انقطاع وهو يتنوع بتنوع المحَالّ، فيكون نوراً في المنوَّر وظُلمة في المُظلم، ولوناً في المتلون، وحركة في المتحرك، وعلماً في العالم، وإرادة في المريد، وحفاظاً في المحفوظ.

فافهم ما أشرنا إليه، ولو (كان) هناك مسك عن موجود ما، لم يكن اسم الجود فيما أعطى بأولى من اسم البخل فيما أمسك!

فمن قال (إنَّ الله تعالى) "لم يُعطِ"، (أو إنَّه هو لم يُعطَ، بفتح الطاء)، فإنه يكذب، فقد أُعطي وهو لا يعلم، وقد أعطاه الجود أن يريد ما لا تقتضي حقيقته - التي هو عليها في الوقت - قبوله، فما هناك منعٌ أصلاً.

٣٥

[الإمام المبين واللوح المحفوظ]

ومنهم من سماه "الإمام المبين" و"اللوح المحفوظ"، قال تعالى: (وَكُلَّ شَيْءٍ أَحْصَيْنَاهُ فِي إِمَامٍ مُبِينٍ) [36: 12]، وهذا الموجود هو الذي أحصي فيه كل شيء، وقال تعالى: (بَلْ هُوَ قُرْآنٌ مَجِيدٌ، فِي لَوْحٍ مَحْفُوظٍ) [85: 21-22]، وهذا الموجود "لوح" من حيث إنه كتب الحقُّ (المخلوق به) فيه "كلَّ شيء"، و"محفوظ" عليه ما عنده من التبديل.

ونزعت طائفة إلى أن "اللوح هو النفس"، وهذا (الموجود الذي هو الجوهر الأول) هو القلم، وسنبين ذلك إن شاء الله تعالى.

وأوصافه كثيرة لا يحصيها إلا خالقها، وكل واحد اعتبر أمراً ما فيه، فأطلق عليه لفظاً من باب ما اعتبر فيه.

[الوجود الأزلي]

فالباري سبحانه هو القديم الأزلي، العالمِ المريد، القادر، الذي لا يمتنع من قدرته ممكن، والموجود لا من عدم. الباقي بنفسه الذي له الكمال المطلق والتمام المحقق.

إِلَّا بِالْحَقِّ) [15: 85].

وإنما سماه "الحقَّ المخلوق به" لكون "الحقّ" من أسماء الله تعالى وليس بمخلوق. ومعنى مخلوق: "موجود عن عدم"، و"مقدر"، وكلاهما صحيح.

[العدل]

ومنهم من سماه "العدل"، وهو الذي ارتضاه أبو عبيد الله سهل بن عبد الله التُستري،[8] فقال إنه روي أنه "بالعدل قامت السموات والأرض"، وقال الله تعالى: (وَأَقِيمُوا الْوَزْنَ بِالْقِسْطِ) [55: 9]، وهو العدل، وقال تعالى: (وَبِالْحَقِّ أَنزَلْنَاهُ وَبِالْحَقِّ نَزَلَ) [17: 105]، أي بالعدل (نزل)، وهو أول من قبل صورة العدل، لأنه عدل عن نفسه إلى باريه تعالى.

---

[8] بو محمد سهل بن عبد الله بن يونس التستري، هو من علماء أهل السنة والجماعة ومن أعلام التصوف السني في القرن الثالث الهجري، وصفه أبو عبد الرحمن السلمي بأنه «أحد أئمة الصوفية وعلمائهم والمتكلمين في علوم الإخلاص والرياضيات وعيوب الأفعال»، أصله من "تستر" أحد مدن محافظة خوزستان الموجودة حالياً في إيران. له كتاب في «تفسير القرآن» وكتاب «رقائق المحبين» وغير ذلك.

الوجه الواحد لكونه روح، أي في نعيم وسرور وراحة، بعلمه بربه، ومشاهدته إياه.

والوجه الآخر أنه راح في فسيحات أفلاك معرفة خالقه، لقوة ما، وراح في مراتب الأكوان بما يُلقي إليها مما وكَّله الله به، وراح في معرفة نفسه بما هو فقير إلى ربه وموجود. فله ثلاث روحات فيمكن أنه سمي لهذا روحا كليا، لأنه ما ثم مرتبة رابعة زائدة على هذه تُراح فيها.

فكأنه أمرٌ من: يروح، والأمر منه: "رح"، فلما نُقل من الأمر إلى الاسم رُدَّت عليه الواو، كما دخلت عليه الألف واللام (للتعريف)، فإنَّ حذف الواو منه لالتقاء الساكنين، فكأنه إذا طلب من جهة قيل راح إلى جهة أخرى، كما ذكرنا.

[الحق المخلوق به]

ومنهم من سماه "الحقَّ المخلوقِ به"، وهو الذي ارتضاه بعض العارفين، وهو أبو الحكم بن برّجان،[7] من قول الله عز وجل: (مَا خَلَقْنَاهُمَا إِلَّا بِالْحَقِّ) [44: 39] وقال: تعالى: (وَبِالْحَقِّ نَزَلَ) [17: 105])، وقوله: (وَمَا خَلَقْنَا السَّمَاوَاتِ وَالْأَرْضَ وَمَا بَيْنَهُمَا

---

[7] هو أبو الحكم عَبْد السَّلام بن عَبْد الرحمن بن محمد اللخمي الإشبيلي، صوفي من الأندلس. من آثاره «شرح أسماء الله الحسنى» وكتاب مشهور في تفسير القرآن تنبَّأ فيه بفتح بيت المقدس في شهر رجب سنة 583 هـ. توفي بمراكش سنة 536 هـ / 1141 م.

[الروح الكلّي]

ومنهم من سماه "الروح الكلّي".

قال الله تعالى: (فَإِذَا سَوَّيْتُهُ وَنَفَخْتُ فِيهِ مِن رُّوحِي) [15: 29]، فأضافه (الله سبحانه وتعالى) إليه إضافة تشريف، لأنه نَفَسُ[7] الباري تعالى، وقال تعالى: (قُلِ الرُّوحُ مِنْ أَمْرِ رَبِّي) [17: 85]، وهذا ما يدلك على أنه يطلب من الله طلب شوق (لأنَّ هذا الروح خرج منه تعالى، كما يخرج النَّفَسُ من المحبِّ، وذلك لأنَّ سبب بدء الخلق هو الحبُّ، كما قال تعالى في الحديث القدسي: «كنت كنزا لم أعرف فأحببت أن أعرف»، فبهذا الحب وقع التنفُّس، فظهر النَّفَسُ، ... الفتوحات المكية ج2 ص310).

[سبب وصفه بالكلّي]

وإنما هو "الكلّي" لأن جميع مقامات العالم محصورة فيه، ومنه تنبعث، وإليه ترجع، وهو السبب الأول لإيجاد الأعيان والأرواح كلها.

[أصل تسميته بالروح الكلي]

وأصل هذا الاسم له من وجهين:

وكذلك الحقائق كلها: صفة وموصوف، وما منه شيء إلا وله مقابله.

[القلم]

ومنهم من سماه أيضاً "القلم".

قال تعالى (ن وَالْقَلَمِ) [68: 1] وقال النبي صلى الله عليه وسلم: «أول ما خلق الله تعالى القلم، وخلق اللوح له فقال له اكتب، فقال يا رب وما أكتب؟» وهذا ما (وال "ما" زائدة، فهذا) يدلُّ على عجزه وافتقاره، «فقال له ربه تعالى: اكتب علمي في خلقي إلى يوم القيامة». لجرى القلم بما أمره به سبحانه.

وهذا يدل على أن القلم كان قد أعلمه الله ذلك (بالتجلي الأول)، وما توقف إلا من حيث (أنّه) لم يدري أيَّ فنٍّ يكتب من فنون العلم الحاصل عنده! فلما عيَّنه (له الله تعالى) جرى على حسب ما علمه (منه بالتجلي الأول)، ولو لم يحتج إلى علم أصلا، فإنّه فائدة لتوالي الفيض عليه (بالتجليات الآنية) واستمراره أبداً!

ثم لتعلم بعد هذا أنه مع هذه المرتبة (الرفيعة من العلم، فهو أعلم الخلق بربِّه، لكنَّه لا يزال) يطلب ربَّه كما تطلبه أنت، ولكن من حيث قُوَّته التي جَبَلَه الله عليها (كونه هو العقل الكلّي)، لا من حيث قوَّتك (أنت بعقلك الجزئي).

[العقل]

فمنهم من سماه "العقل".

قال رسول الله صلى الله عليه وسلم «أول ما خلق الله العقل، فقال له أقبل فأقبل ثم قال له أدبر فأدبر»، فأقبل للاستفادة وأدبر بالإفادة.

ولكنَّ إدبارَه إقبالٌ، وذلك أنَّ الاسم الذي قال له أقبل فأقبل، ثم قال له أدبر فأدبر، فـ (لمّا أدبر) أخذه اسم آخر (فهو دائماً مُقبل، وإنَّما إلى أسماء متوالية).

وإنما أعطي في أول (نسبة) نشأة الإقبال والإدبار، لكون الوجود عليهما أنبنى، وهما القبضتان (وذلك من حديث: «إن الله قبض قبضتين، فقال: هذه للجنة ولا أبالي، وهذه للنار ولا أبالي») والحقيقتان الحاكمتان على العالم بالسعادة والشقاوة.

ومن هذا الإقبال والإدبار ظهرت: الجنة والنار، والقبض والبسط، والألم واللذة، والعدم والوجود.

فإنه ليس إلا اثنان، وكل ما زاد على اثنين فإنه يرجع إلى الاثنين، ولا بد، إذا نظرت فيه.

وكذلك الثلاثة وغيرها، فاعلم ذلك.

(غير أنَّ الاثنين أيضاً ترجع إلى الواحد، لأنه هو الأول والآخر والظاهر والباطن، فما ثَمَّ إلا واحد!)

فإن الوجود كلَّه محصورٌ في حقيقة القبض (التي تلي البسط).

ولهذا خرج النبي صلى الله عليه وسلم بالكآبين.

فلا يزال يُجدَّد له ذلك، ولهذا لا يزال الباري تعالى خالقا في الدنيا والآخرة.

[العقل الأول]

ثم اعلم أن الله تعالى لما أوجد هذا العقل، وهو جوهر فرد قائم بنفسه، متحيز في مذهب، وغير متحيِّز في مذهب، وهو الأصح؛ تجلى له بذاته فأفاض عليه المعلومات كلها، فعلمه متعلق بجميع المعلومات إلا علمه بالله تعالى، فإنَّه ما أحاط به علماً البتة، لكن لا يزال الله تعالى يفيض العلم عليه منه أبداً، وهو يقبل، وبهذا يُطلق عليه "الاستفادة" (من التجليات الآنية من الله تعالى) لا مِن جهة علوم الكون، فإنه قد علِمها (بالتجلي الأول)، ومحال أن يعلم الله تعالى على الإطلاق.

وقد أشار إلى هذا صلى الله عليه وسلم، فقال: «إني أسألك بكل اسم سميت به نفسك، أو علَّمته أحداً من خلقك، أو استأثرت به في علم غيبك». فقوله: "أو استأثرت به"، هي ما أردنا.

[أسماء الجوهر الفرد]

فهذا الموجود (الذي نحن في صدده، وهو الجوهر الأول) اختلفت الأسماء عليه والألقاب:

والممكن هو الذي يُتصوَّر عدمُه ووجودُه على السواء، من غير ترجيحٍ لنفسه. فإنه لو رجَّح لنفسه الوجودَ على العدم، لم يخل أنه يرجح نفسه (حالَ ترجيحها) وهو "موجود" أو "معدوم": فإن رجَّح وجودَه وهو موجود فما الذي رجَّح؟ ومن المحال أن يرجِّح وجودَه وهو معدوم، فإن المعدوم ليس بشيء فلا يتصور حكمٌ منه عقلا!

فإذا رأينا قد ترجَّح له (أي للممكن) أحد الجائزين (وهما الوجود أو العدم)، علمنا أن ذلك من مشيئة مرجِّحه، وأنَّ مرجِّحَه لا بدَّ أن يكون واجبَ الوجود (وهو الباري سبحانه وتعالى)، مريداً لإيجاد هذا الممكن.

والواجبُ الوجود هو الذي لا يُتصوَّر عدمُه عقلاً، كما أن المحال لا يُتصور وجودُه عقلا.

وليس يلزم من كون المشيئة واجبة الوجود أن هذا الممكن الذي تعلقت به لم يزل معها، فيكون أزليا بأزليتها، هذا لا يلزم. فإن الإرادة قد ثبت لها أنها لا تتعلق إلا بمعدوم، فإذا وُجد المعدوم لم تتعلق الإرادة به من كونه موجود، فقد ثبت له العدم أصلاً، وإنما تتعلق عند وجوده ببقاء وجوده، وهو معدوم، أو بعدمه في الزمان الثاني، زماناً مقدراً أو واقعاً، أي زمان كان وهو معدوم، فإن العين موجودة، ولا بد أن يكون كل ممكن وجوده عن عدم أصلا.

وكذلك القدرة؛ يزول تعلقها بالموجود، لأنها إنما تتعلق لتُوجد، وما بقي تعلق لهذا الموجود إلا بخلق الأعراض التي بها بقاؤه،

أَصْحَابُ النَّارِ هُمْ فِيهَا خَالِدُونَ [البقرة: 257]).

ولا بدَّ أن يكون المرجِّح غير ممكن مثله، لكون الممكن (هو بحد ذاته معدوم و) يفتقر إلى مرجِّح، وذلك محال (أن يكون المرجِّح ممكن الوجود، لأنه في الحقيقة معدوم، وذلك) لأن المعدوم لا يرجِّح شيئاً، فلا بدَّ أن يكون المرجِّحُ واجبَ الوجود لنفسه، وهو الله سبحانه (ولا أحد غيره واجب الوجود لنفسه).

ولا يصح أن يكون هذا الممكن واجبَ الوجود بالله، تعالى، فيكون معه أزلاً، والممكن يستحيل وجودُه أزلاً، لأنه لا فائدة لواجب الوجود إلا أن يكون "لا عن عدم".

وحقيقة الممكن لا تقبل الوجوب العقلي، ولا تقبل الوجوب المقيد، الذي يُقال عنه "واجبٌ بغيره"، ومن المحال تعلُّق الإرادة بالموجود، وإنما تتعلق بالمعدوم، وإذا تعلقت ببقاء الموجود لم يقع، فهو مستأنف. (وهذه مسألة عويصة بحاجة إلى بعض الشرح والتفصيل؛ فكما قلنا أعلاه: وجود الممكن آني لا يدوم، ولا بدَّ من تجديد الخلق عليه، فيظهر بوجود جديد في كل آن. فالإرادة تنقله من العدم إلى الوجود، ولا تنقله من الوجود إلى العدم، لأن ذلك واقع من غير فعل فاعل، كما قال الشيخ في بداية الفتوحات إن "فعل لا شيء" لا يقول به عاقل، فالفعل لا يُنتج العدم، بل هو صفة لازمة لكل موجود غير الله سبحانه وتعالى. وهذا يعني أنه لا بقاء لموجودٍ [مخلوق] بعينه، بل بقاؤه بتجدد الأعراض عليه، وزوالها في كل آن، وعينه لا تزال ثابتة على حالها في الإمكان.)

[الوجود الممكن]

ثم قال قدس سره[5]:

فلا بدَّ أن يكون وجود هذا الممكن عن عدم (إمكاني)، يعني (له ابتداء في الزمان، لأنه) لم يكن، ثمَّ كان، فإن الممكن هو الذي ليس في حقيقته أن يمتنع من الوجود، كالمحال (وهو العدم المطلق، الذي لا يُتخيَّل وجوده: مثل وجود شريك لله سبحانه وتعالى عن ذلك علوًّا كبيرا!)، ولا من العدم (المطلق)، كالواجب (الذي لا يُتخيل عدمه، مثل وجود الله سبحانه وتعالى)؛ فهو (أي الممكن) جائزٌ أن يكون موجوداً وجائزٌ أن يكون معدوماً، وجائزٌ إذا كان موجوداً أن يُعدم، وجائزٌ إذا كان معدوماً أن يوجد، فيفتقر بالضرورة إلى المرجِّح (لكي يخرجه من ظلمة العدم الإمكاني إلى نور الوجود النسبي، كما قال الله تعالى: اللَّهُ وَلِيُّ الَّذِينَ آمَنُوا يُخْرِجُهُم مِّنَ الظُّلُمَاتِ إِلَى النُّورِ وَالَّذِينَ كَفَرُوا أَوْلِيَاؤُهُمُ الطَّاغُوتُ يُخْرِجُونَهُم مِّنَ النُّورِ إِلَى الظُّلُمَاتِ أُولَٰئِكَ

---

[5] يتضح من هذه العبارة أن هذا الكتاب منقول من كلام الشيخ محي الدين، وليس هو من كتبه. ويعزز ذلك أيضاً العنوان الكامل لهذا الكتاب، وهو: "جواب عن مسألة الدرة البيضاء" أي إن الشيخ قال هذا الكلام إجابة على سؤال، فربما قام السائل أو أحد التلاميذ بتدوين هذا الجواب كما سمعه من الشيخ محي الدين. من أجل ذلك أيضاً نجد أن بعض العبارات أقرب إلى الحديث العام منها إلى النص المنسق والمدقق.

[6] العبارة من " أي إنَّه مفتقر..." إلى هنا، سقطت من المخطوطات.

فإنه (إذا صح وجودُه المطلق): كان لا يكون ممكنًا، وهو ممكن، وكان لا يكون موجوداً لهذا الواجب، وهو موجود له، ولم يعمل فيه سوى إيجاد عينه؛ أي إنَّه مفتقر إليه، تعالى، في "إيجاد عينه"، لا في "عينه"،[3] لأنَّ "عينه الثابتة"[4] غير مجعولة في ثبوتها، فليست بجعل جاعل، إذ لا جَعْلَ في الأزل.

كيف يصح ذلك وهو الذي افتتح الفتوحات بقوله: "الحمد لله الذي أوجد الأشياء عن عدم".

[3] لعلَّ هذا الفارق الدقيق، الموضح هنا، هو السبب في إساءة فهم الكثير من عبارات الشيخ الأكبر والتي كثيرا ما تكون مختصرة ودقيقة، وخاصة في كتاب فصوص الحكم. فالموجودات مفتقرة إلى الباري سبحانه في إيجاد أعيانها من العدم (الإمكاني) إلى الوجود (الآني)، وأما الأعيان بحد ذاتها فهي ثابتة في علمه سبحانه، وعلمه غير محدث، فبهذا لا تكون الأعيان مفتقرة إلى الخالق، ولكن لا نقول إنها غنية عن الخالق، بل لا ينطلق عليها الغنى والفقر لأنها ثابتة في الأزل، وما طرأ عليها سوى وجودها الآني من عدمها الإمكاني. من أجل ذلك لا بدَّ أن يكون الوجود آنيا، إذ لو استمرَّ وجود العين زمانين لكانت غنية عن الإيجاد، وهذا لا يكون، فالأعيان ثابتة في الإمكان، والأعراض زائلة في الآن. ومن هنا كذلك يمكن فهم سر الأزل الذي أشار إليه الشيخ في كتاب الأزل، حيث قال إن (في الأزل نكتة عجيبة، وهو أن العالم لما ظهر بدعوى الظهور أراد الحق أن يطمسه بأزليته؛ فلا يبقى للمحدث أثر. فتجلى "أزل" ففني العالم بظهور الألف من "أزل" خاصة، وبقي "زل"، في حق العالم: كأن سائلاً سأل أين العالم؟ فقيل له: زلَّ بظهور ألف الذات! والألف هي المطلوبة من الأزل خاصة من أجل الأحدية.). فالألف في تجل دائم، والكون في زوال لازم، لا يدوم سوى زمن وجوده، وهو زمن فرد، غير ممتد، فهو لا يدوم أبداً.

[4] فكرة الأعيان الثابتة ..

٢٤

الدرة البيضاء

بسم الله الرحمن الرحيم
وبه ثقتي

[الوجود الواجب]

اعلم أن الله، سبحانه وتعالى، هو الوجود المطلق، لا عن عدم، بل وجب وجوده لنفسه؛ فلم يزل موجوداً، ولا يزال واحداً في ذاته. له الأسماء الحُسنى، والصفات العُلى، ولا يتعدد بأسمائه وصفاته.

فإنَّ الواحد، بذاته، لا يتعدد بما يقوم به من المعاني. وإنما تتعدد الذات القائمة بنفسها بكونها تقبل القسمة؛ فتكون ذات أجزاء، فيدخلها العد.

والصفة ليست بجزء لموصوفها.

وهو سبحانه ليس بمادة، ولا في مادة، بل هو غنيٌّ، قائمٌ بنفسه، غيرُ متحيِّز، ولا قابلٌ للحَدَثان (في 1821: للمُحدثات).

فثبت وجودُه، تعالى، ولا عينَ موجودةٌ سواه.

فكل ما سواه فهو موجودٌ به، وهو فعلُه، وخَلقُه، وصنعتُه، ووجود ما هو موجود موقوفٌ على إرادته، التي هي مشيئته، سبحانه، وقدرته، وسابق علمه.

ولا يصح أن يكون الموجود المقيَّد موجوداً إلا عن عدم،²

---

² من هنا تتضح فداحة من يتهم الشيخ الأكبر بأنه يقول بقدم العالم،

الّتي لا تنفد... ولهذا الملك الكريم (الذي هو اللوح أو النفس) نسبتان نسبة نورانيّة وهو ممّا يلي العقل الكريم ونسبة ظلمانيّة وهو ممّا يلي الهباء، بحر الطبيعة، وهي في نفسها خضراء لهذا الامتزاج الدقيق العجيب، وقد استوفينا ذكرها وصفتها في كتاب النفس وهو كتاب الزمرّدة الخضراء، وذكرنا أيضا مقام القلم الأعلى في كتاب مفرد سمّيناه "الدّرّة البيضاء".

وفيما يلي نص كتاب الدرة البيضاء، للشيخ الأكبر محي الدين ابن العربي، رضي الله عنه، مع بعض التعليقات والشروحات المضافة من قبل المترجم.

يتناهى، وطريقة علمه به التجليّات، وطريقة علمه بربّه علمُهُ به. ويُقبل على مَن دونه مفيداً، هكذا أبد الآباد في المزيد. فهو الفقير الغنيّ، العزيز الذليل، العبد السيّد، ولا يزال الحقّ يلهمُه طلب التجليّات لتحصيل المعارف. [عقلة المستوفز، باب في خلق العقل الأوّل]

وقال في نفس هذا الكتاب في باب في العرش العظيم، وهو اللوح المحفوظ وهو النفس الناطقة الكلّيّة الثابتة:

ولمّا أوجد الله سبحانه القلم الأعلى، أوجد له في المرتبة الثانية هذه النفس الّتي هي اللوح المحفوظ، ... فأمر القلم أن يجرى على هذا اللوح بما قدّره وقضاه ممّا كان من إيجاده. ... فهذا اللوح محلّ الإلقاء العقليّ هو للعقل بمنزلة حوّاء لآدم عليه السلام، وسمّيت نفسا لأنّها وجدت من نفس الرحمن، فنفّس الله، بها عن العقل إذ جعلها محلاًّ لقبول ما يُلقى إليه ولوحاً لما يسطره فيه. ... وهذا القلم له ثلاثمائة وستّون سنًّا، من حيث ما هو القلم، وثلاثمائة وستّون وجه ونسبة من حيث ما هو عقل، و ثلاثمائة وستّون لسانا من حيث ما هو روح مترجم عن الله. ويستمدّ كلّ سنّ من ثلاثمائة وستّين بحر، وهي أصناف العلوم، وسمّيت بحرا لاتّساعها، و هذه البحور هي إجمال الكلمات

عالم التدوين والتسطير، وهو الخازن الحفيظ العليم الأمين على اللطائف الإنسانيّة الّتي من أجلها وُجد ولها قُصد. ميّزها في ذاته عن سائر الأرواح تمييزاً إلهيًّا. عَلِم نفسَه، فعَلِم موجدَه، فعَلِم العالَمَ، فعَلِم الإنسان.

قال رسول الله صلّى الله عليه وسلّم: "من عرف نفسه عرف ربه"، لسانَ إجمال. والحديث الآخر: "أعرفكم بنفسه أعرفكم بربّه"، لسانَ تفصيل.

فهو العقل من هذا الوجه، وهو القلم من حيث التدوين والتسطير، وهو الروح من حيث التصرّف، وهو العرش من حيث الاستواء، وهو الإمام المبين من حيث الإحصاء.

ورقائقه الّتي تمتدّ إلى النفس، إلى الهباء، إلى الجسم، إلى الأفلاك الثابتة، إلى المركز، إلى الأركان؛ بالصعود إلى الأفلاك المستحيلة، إلى الحركات، إلى المولّدات، إلى الإنسان، إلى انعقادها في العنصر الأعظم، وهو أصلها: ستّة وأربعون ألف ألف رقيقة وسّمائة ألف رقيقة وستّة وخمسون ألف رقيقة، ولا يزال هذا العقل متردّدا بين الإقبال والإدبار، يُقبل على باريه مستفيداً، فيتجلّى له فيكشف في ذاته من بعض ما هو عليه، فيعلم من باريه قدر ما عَلِم من نفسه؛ فعلمه بذاته لا يتناهى، فعلمه بربّه لا

له الإمساك عنه، فإذا ظهر عين الكلام في الوجود ففيضه على الأسماع ذاتيّ لا إراديّ. [المسائل، مسألة رقم 10 في طبعة دار الكتب العلمية، 2001، ص 307]

وقد ذكر الشيخ هذه الوجوه التي للعقل الأول في كتاب عقلة المستوفز، فقال:

باب في خلق العقل الأوّل، وهو القلم الأعلى: فأوّل ما أوجد الله من عالم العقول المدبّرة جوهراً بسيطاً، ليس بمادّة، ولا في مادّة، عالمٌ بذاته في ذاته. علمُه ذاتُه، لا صفة له، مقامه الفقرُ والذلّة والاحتياج إلى باريه وموجوده ومبدعه. له نسب وإضافات ووجوه كثيرة، لا يتكثّر في ذاته بتعدّده. فيّاضٌ بوجهين من الفيض: فيضٌ ذاتيّ وفيض إراديّ، فما هو بالذات مطلقاً لا يتّصف بالمنع في ذلك، وما هو بالإرادة فإنّه يوصف فيه بالمنع وبالعطاء. وله افتقارٌ ذاتيٌّ لموجده سبحانه، الّذي استفاد منه وجوده، وسمّاه الحقُّ سبحانه وتعالى في القرآن: "حقّاً" و "قلماً" و "روحاً"، وفي السنّة: "عقلاً"، وغير ذلك من الأسماء. قد ذكرنا أكثرها في كثير من كتبنا.

قال الله تعالى (وَمَا خَلَقْنَا السَّمَاوَاتِ وَالْأَرْضَ وَمَا بَيْنَهُمَا إِلَّا بِالْحَقِّ) [15: 85]، وهو أوّل

العالَم، فهو على الصورة. والروحانيات أقوى على الكمال من عالَم الأجسام، لاستعدادهم الأكمل، ولهذا يرغب البشر في تحصيل القوة الروحانية بالطبع، فمنهم من وصل فكمل، ومنهم من لم يصل لموانع عرضية وأصلية في هذا الدار. وأما في الدار الآخرة فالكل يصل إليها، ويقع الامتياز بينهم بأمور أُخَر ترجع إلى الصورة التي يدخلون فيها.

فلما أُوجِد هذا الموجود الأول، ظهر له من الوجوه إلى الحضرة الإلهية ثلثمائة وستين وجهاً، فأفاض الحق تعالى عليه من علمه على قدر ما أوجده عليه من الاستعداد للقبول، فكان قبوله ستة وأربعين ألف نوع وسّمائة ألف نوع وستة آلاف وخمسين ألف نوع (وذلك لأنَّ له وجوه ثلاثة، فيكون: $360 \times 360 \times 360 = 46656000$)، فظهرت لهذا العقل أحكام تعددها لا غير، ونَشَر منها في كلِّ عالَم بما يستحق، نَشْرَ إفاضة لا نَشْرَ اختيار، فإنَّ وجوهه مصروفة إلى مُوجِدِه، والعالَم يستمدون من ذاته بحسب قُواهم، كقبول عالَم الأكوان لنور الشمس، من غير إرادة الشمس في ذلك؛ وهذا الفرق بين الفيض الذاتي والفيض الإرادي، ذلك راجع لنفس المُفيض. ألا ترون إلى فيض العالِم كلامه على الأسماع: إراديّ، لأنَّ

العقلي) في ذلك النظر، فيُدخَلُ عليه بما قد ذكرناه في "عيون المسائل" في "مسألة الدرة البيضاء" الذي هو العقل الأوَّل، وهذا الذي ذكرناه لا يلزم عليه دخل، فإنَّا ما ادَّعيناه نظراً، وإنَّما ادَّعيناه تعريفاً، فغاية المنكر أن يقول للقائل: "تكذبّ" ليس له غير ذلك، كما يقول له المؤمن به: "صدقت"، فهذا فرقانٌ بيننا وبين (الفلاسفة) القائلين بالاعتبارات الثلاثة (التي للعقل)، وبالله التوفيق. [الفتوحات المكية: ج1 ص46]

كذلك ورد ذكر "الدرَّة البيضاء" في كتاب المعرفة، وهو كتاب المسائل التي اقتبس منه الشيخ محي الدين في مقدمة الفتوحات، فقال:

مسألة: فأوَّل موجودٍ ظهر، مقيَّدٍ، فقيرٍ، موجودٌ يُسمَّى "العقل الأوَّل"، ويُسمَّى "الروح الكلي"، ويسمى "القلم"، ويسمى "العدل"، ويسمى "العرش"، ويسمى "الحق المخلوق به"، ويسمى "الحقيقة المحمدية"، ويسمى "روح الأرواح"، ويسمى "الإمام المبين"، ويسمى "كلَّ شيء"، وله أسماء كثيرة باعتبار ما فيه من الوجوه. وهو على نصف الصورة المعلومة عندنا، سمعاً وكشفاً، في وجه، وعلى الصورة في وجه آخر، على حسب ما يقع تجليه، لأنَّ العالَمَ كلَّه على الصورة، والإنسانُ من العالمَ على صورة

العالَم، المنفعل عن الزمردة الخضراء. فإن قلت: وما الزمردة الخضراء؟ قلنا: النفْس، المنبعثة عن الدرة البيضاء. فإن قلت: وما الدرة البيضاء؟ قلنا: العقل الأول".

كذلك قال الشيخ الأكبر في مقدمته للفتوحات:

كنَّا حصرنا في كتاب المعرفة الأول ما للعقل من وجوه المعارف في العالَم، ولم ننبِّه من أين حصل لنا ذلك الحصر! فاعلم أنَّ للعقل ثلاثمائة وستين وجهاً، يقابل كلُّ وجهٍ من جناب الحق العزيز ثلاثمائة وستين وجهاً، يمدُّهُ كلُّ وجهٍ منها بعلم لا يُعطيه الوجه الآخر. فإذا ضربت وجوهَ العقل في وجوهِ الأخْذِ، فالخارج من ذلك هي العلوم التي للعقل، المسطَّرَة في اللَّوح المحفوظ، الذي هو النفْس. وهذا الذي ذكرناه كشفاً إلهيًّا لا يُحيله دليل عقل، فيُتَلقَّى تسليماً من قائله، أعني هذا كما تَلقَّى من القائل الحكيم (يعني الفلاسفة الذين يقولون بالفيض، وبـ) الثلاثة الاعتبارات، التي للعقل الأوَّل، من غير دليل، لكن مصادرةً (وهذه المسألة يناقشها الشيخ في هذا الكتاب الذي بين أيدينا، والذي يشير إليه هنا باسم "عيون المسائل"). فهذا أولى من ذلك، فإنَّ الحكيم يدَّعي (الدَّليلَ

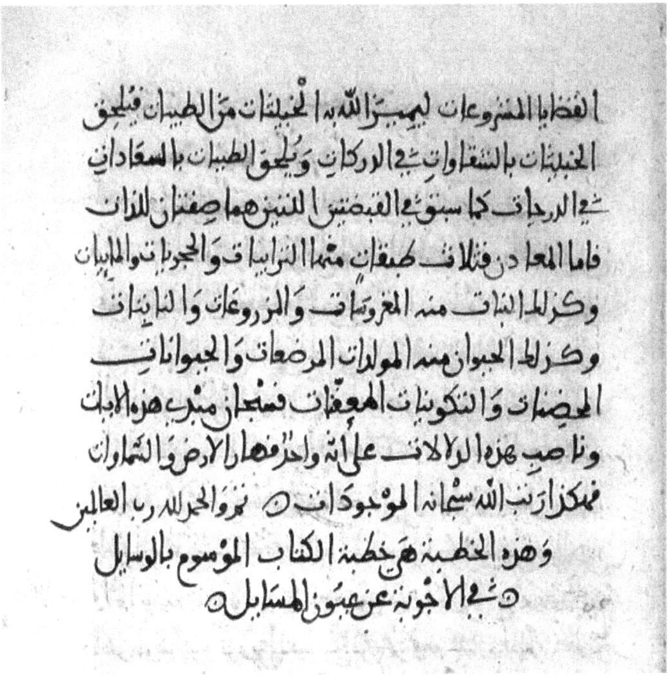

القضايا المشروعات ليميز الله به الخبيثات من الطيبات فيلحق
الخبيثات بالشقاوات في الدركات ويلحق الطيبات بالسعادات
في الدرجات كما سبق في القبضتين اللتين هما صفتان للذات
فاما المعادن فثلاث طبقات منها الترابيات والحجريات والمائيات
وكذلك النبات منه المغروسات والمزروعات والنابتات
وكذلك الحيوان منه المولدات المرضعات والحيوانات
المحيضات والتكوينيات المعفنات فسبحان من رتب هذه الآيات
ونصب هذه الدلالات على انه واحد فصار الارض والسماوات
فمكن ان ترتب الله سبحانه الموجودات ○ تم والحمد لله رب العالمين
وهذه الخطبة هي خطبة الكتاب الموسوم بالوسايل
في الاجوبة عن عيون المسايل ○

شكل ٦: نهاية مخطوطة الخطبة من مجموع يوسف أغا 4868، والتي يبدو أنها مكتوبة بخط الشيخ الأكبر.

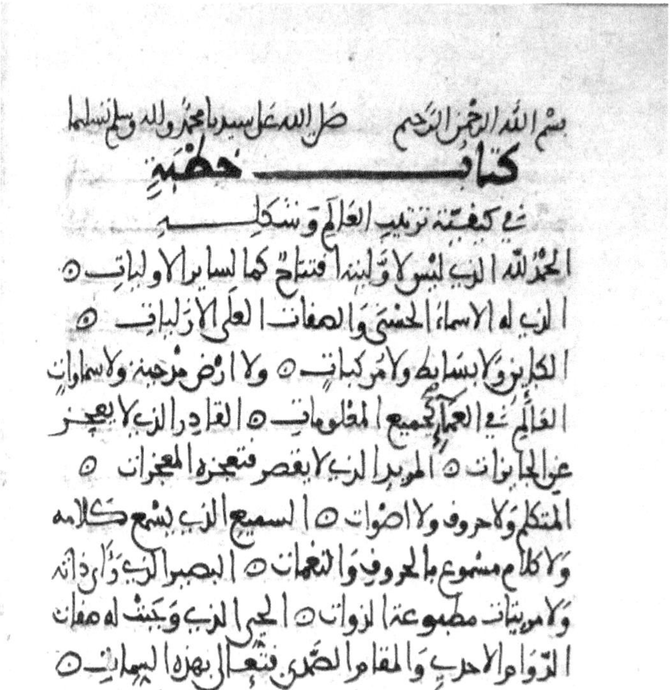
بسم الله الرحمن الرحيم صلى الله على سيدنا محمد وآله وسلم تسليما
كتاب خطبة
في كيفية ترتيب العالم وشكله
الحمد لله الذي ليس لأوليته افتتاح كما لسائر الأوليات ○
الذي له الأسماء الحسنى والصفات العلى الأزليات ○
الكائن ولا بسائط ولا مركبات ○ ولا أرض مدحية ولا سماوات
العالم في العماء بجميع المخلوقات ○ القادر الذي لا يعجز
عن الجائزات ○ المريد الذي لا يقصر فتعجزه المعجزات ○
المتكلم ولا حروف ولا أصوات ○ السميع الذي يسمع كلامه
ولا كلام مسموع بالحروف والنغمات ○ البصير الذي يرى ذاته
ولا مرئيات مطبوعة الذوات ○ الحي الذي وجبت له صفات
الدوام الأحدي والمقام الصمدي فتعالى بهذه الصفات ○
الذي جعل الإنسان أشرف الموجودات وأتم الكلمات ○

شكل ٥: بداية مخطوطة الخطبة من مجموع يوسف أغا 4868، والتي يبدو أنها مكتوبة بخط الشيخ الأكبر.

في مكتبة برلين (تحت رقم 2960 و 3001) تضمان مسألة الزمرّدة والسبحة، ولم نستطع الاطلاع عليهما.

وأما كتاب المسائل الثلاث، فله مخطوطة في مجموع أولو جامع 1619، وهي نسخة قديمة.

وأما بالنسبة لكتاب "عيون المسائل"، والذي يمكن أن يكون هو الكتاب الأم الذي يضم هذه المسائل الثلاث، فله مخطوطات كثيرة، ولكنها غير كاملة وهي في الأغلب لا تحوي سوى المقدمة أو خطبة الكتاب المسماة: "خطبة في نضد العالم". من هذه المخطوطات: بغدادلي 714، نافز 685، فينّا 1910، إضافة إلى مخطوطة يوسف أغا 4868، والتي يبدو أنها مكتوبة بخط الشيخ الأكبر، وهي ضمن مكتبة القونوي الخاصة. وقد وضعنا أيضاً بداية ونهاية هذه المخطوطة ضمن اللوحات المرفقة.

ولا بدَّ لنا هنا من التوجُّه بالشكر الجزيل والعرفان للأخ الكريم أبو أحمد محمد كابر الأنصاري الذي زوَّدنا ببعض هذه المخطوطات وأفادنا بمعلوماته القيّمة من خلال مناقشات مطوَّلة وملاحظات مهمة عن أصول هذه الكتب المتداخلة للشيخ محي الدين والمخطوطات المختلفة لها.

[ذكره في الفتوحات المكية والكتب الأخرى]

أثناء أجوبته على أسئلة الحكيم الترمذي، يقول الشيخ محي الدين في الجزء الثاني من الفتوحات المكية (ج2 ص130): "فإن قلت: وما السبحة؟ قلنا: الهباء، الذي فتح فيه صور أجسام

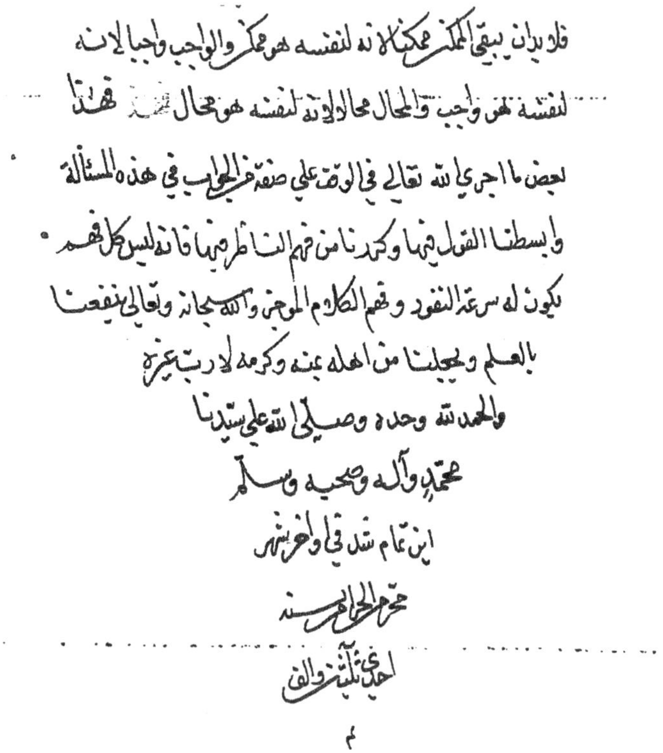

فلا بد إن يبقى الممكن ممكنا لانه لنفسه هو ممكن والواجب واجبا لانه لنفسه لفى واجب والمحال لا لانه لنفسه هو محال فهذا بعض ما اجرى الله تعالى في الوقت على صفة من الجواب في هذه المسألة وبسطنا القول فيها وكررنا من تتم النا ظر فيها فانه ليس كل فهم يكون له سرعة النفوذ وفهم الكلام الموجز والله سبحانه وتعالى ينفعنا بالعلم ويجعلنا من اهله عنده وكرمه لا رب غيره والحمد لله وحده وصلى الله على سيدنا
محمد وآله وصحبه وسلم
ابن تمام شد فيا واخر شهر
محرم الحرام سنه
احدى ثلثين والف

شكل ٤: نهاية المخطوطة الثانية.

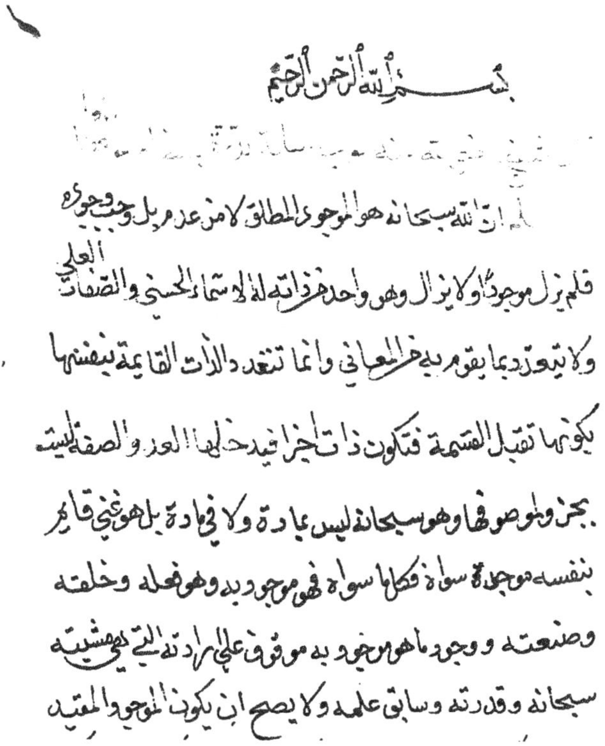

بسم الله الرحمن الرحيم

... ان الله سبحانه هو الموجود المطلق لا من عدم بل وجوده العلي
فلم يزل موجوداً ولا يزال وهو أحدٌ بذاته لذاته اسماؤه الحسنى والصفات
ولا يتعدد بما يقوم بذاته من المعاني وإنما تتعدد الذات القائمة بنفسها
كونها تقبل القسمة فتكون ذا تأخر فيدخلها العدد والصفة ليست
جزء ولموصوفها وهو سبحانه ليس بمادة ولا في مادة بل هو غني قائم
بنفسه موجد سواه فكل ما سواه فهو موجود بدء وهو فعله وخلقه
وصنعته ووجود ما هو موجود به موقوف على إرادته التي هي مشيئته
سبحانه وقدرته وسابق علمه ولا يصح ان يكون الموجود المقيد

شكل ٣: بداية المخطوطة الثانية.

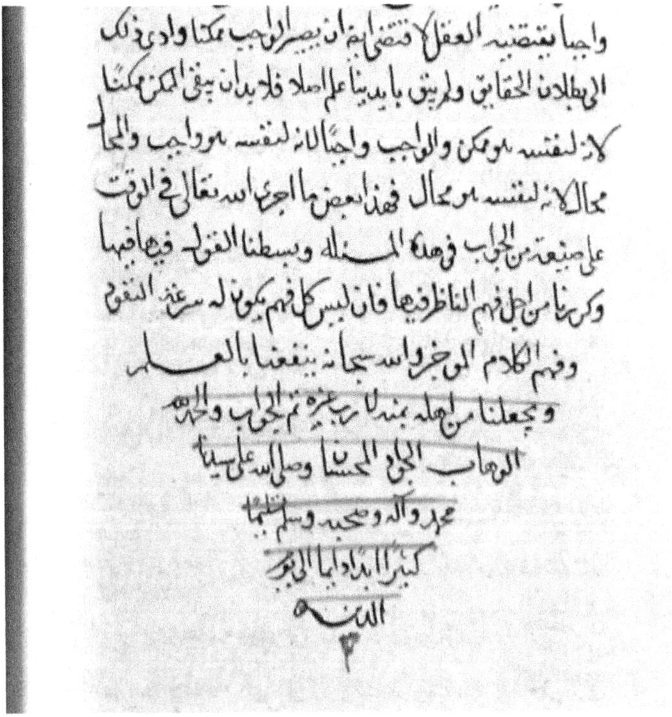

واجبا يقتضيه العقل لا تقتضي به ان يصير الواجب ممكنا وادى ذلك
الى بطلان الحقائق ولم يبق بايدينا علم اصلا فلا بد ان يبقى الممكن ممكنا
لانه لنفسه هو ممكن والواجب واجبا لانه لنفسه هو واجب والمحال
محالا لانه لنفسه هو محال فهذا بعض ما اجراه الله تعالى في الوقت
على صنيعة من الجواب في هذه المسئلة وبسطنا القول فيها فيها
وكررنا من اجل فهم الناظر فيها فانه ليس كل فهم يكون له سرعة النفوذ
وفهم الكلام الموجز والله سبحانه ينفعنا بالعلم
ويجعلنا من اهله بمنه لا رب غيره تم الجواب والحمد لله
الوهاب الجواد المحسن وصلى الله على سيدنا
محمد واله وصحبه وسلم تسليما
كثيرا ابدا دايما الى يوم
الدين

شكل ٢: نهاية مخطوطة ولي الدين 1821.

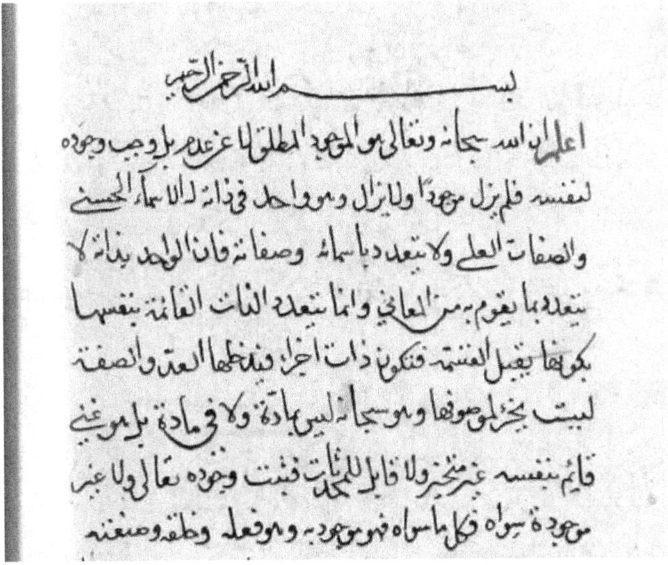
بسم الله الرحمن الرحيم

اعلم ان الله سبحانه وتعالى هو الموجود المطلق لا عن عدم بل وجب وجوده لنفسه فلم يزل موجودا ولا يزال وهو واحد في ذاته له الاسماء الحسنى والصفات العلى ولا يتعدد باسمائه وصفاته فان الواحد بذاته لا يتعدد بما يقوم به من المعاني وانما يتعدد الذات القائمة بنفسها بكونها يقبل القسمة فتكون ذات اجزاء فيدخلها العدد والصفة ليست بجزء للموصوف وهو سبحانه ليس بمادة ولا في مادة بل هو غني قائم بنفسه غير متحيز ولا قابل للمحدثات فثبت وجوده تعالى ولا غير موجود سواه فكل ما سواه فهو موجود به وهو فعله وخلقه وصنعته

شكل ١: بداية مخطوطة ولي الدين 1821.

الماضية، بعد نهاية الألف الهجري.

من ضمن هذه المخطوطات، نسخة جيدة مكتوبة بخط حديث واضح تقع في مجموع "ولي الدين 1821" من الصفحة 238 إلى 244، وهي التي اعتمدنا عليها في هذه الطبعة. ونبيّن في الصور المرفقة بداية ونهاية هذه المخطوطة.

كذلك قارنَّا النص مع مخطوطة أخرى لم نستطع التأكد من مصدرها، ولكنها مكتوبة بخط جميل وواضح، ومؤرخة بتاريخ شهر محرم سنة 1031 هـ، وهي متوافقة بشكل جيد مع المخطوطة السابقة، ونبيّن في الصور المرفقة بداية ونهاية هذه المخطوطة.

وأما مخطوط مكة المكرمة الذي يحمل الرقم 3939، فهو يتضمَّن كذلك الرسائل الثلاث، ولكنَّه مكتوب بخط مضغوط وغير واضح في بعض المواضع.

وهناك مخطوطة أخرى ضمن مجموع: "إسماعيل صائب 1197" (الرسالة الثانية)، لم نتمكن من مطالعتها. وكذلك مخطوطة أخرى في دار الكتب الوطنية في تونس، تحمل الرقم 8572 الصادقية. وكذلك مخطوطة مكتبة الأوقاف العامة في بغداد، الذي يحمل الرقم 7071 مجاميع. وكذلك مخطوطة في مكتبة الأميرة فايزة، مكتبة جامعة الإسكندرية، الذي يحمل الرقم 154561، وهو كذلك يضم جواب الزمردة الخضراء والسبحة السوداء. وكذلك مخطوطة دار الكتب المصرية، مجاميع طلعت 790، وهو بعنوان "المسائل الثلاث: العقل، والنفس، والهيولى"، لكنَّ بدايته ونهايته تتفق تماماً مع مخطوطة ولي الدين، ويبدو أنَّ الدكتور محمد عزب اعتمد على هذه النسخة كما ذكرنا أعلاه. وكذلك هناك نسختان

[الطبعات السابقة]

أول طبعة معروفة لكتاب "الدرَّة البيضاء" ظهرت في القاهرة، وكذلك في بيروت، سنة 1923. وهناك نسخة حديثة متداولة طبعت سنة 1993، من قبل مكتبة مدبولي، بتحقيق الدكتور محمد زينهم محمد عزب، وقال إنه اعتمد على بعض الطبعات القديمة (دون أن يذكرها، وربما تكون هي طبعة 1923) وعلى مخطوطة موجودة في دار الكتب المصرية (دون أن يذكرها كذلك، وربما تكون نسخة "مجاميع طلعت 790" التي سنذكرها بعد قليل). لكن هذا التحقيق يحوي بعض الأخطاء التي تخلِّ بالنص، مع أنه كذلك يحوي بعض الجمل الأساسية الغير موجودة في المخطوطات الأخرى التي اطلعنا عليها.

كذلك ظهر هذا الكتاب مؤخراً في مجموعة "تحرير البيان في تقرير شعب الايمان ورتب الإحسان، رسالة ماهية القلب، وجواب عن مسألة الدرة البيضاء"، بتحقيق الأستاذ الدكتور محمد فاروق صالح البدري، والذي طبع في بغداد سنة 2017، من قبل دار سطور.

[مخطوطات الكتاب]

أما بالنسبة للمخطوطات، فلا توجد من هذا الكتاب أي مخطوطات قديمة، أصلية أو منقولة عن أصل. لكن هناك العديد من المخطوطات الجيدة، التي تبدو أنها مكتوبة في القرون القليلة

سودكين سنة 646 هـ / 1248 م.

الجواب عن الأرواح، إن شاء الله تعالى"، مما يعني أنَّ هناك جزءًا آخر (يتضمَّن الجواب عن الروح) لهذا الكتاب الذي يتضمَّن هذه الأجوبة الثلاثة، عن العقل والنفس والجسم، وهي الدرَّة والزمرّدة والسُّبحة.

ثم نجد كذلك أن بعض هذه الأجوبة مذكورة أيضاً بشكل متفرق ومختصر في "كتاب المعرفة"، أو: "المعرفة في المسائل الاعتقادية"، وكذلك يسمَّى: "عقيدة أهل الاختصاص"، ويبدو أن كتاب "المسائل"، والذي يسمَّى أحياناً: "المسائل في إيضاح المسائل"، هو اختصار لكتاب المعرفة في المسائل الاعتقادية.

وتجدر الإشارة كذلك إلى أنَّ الشيخ إسماعيل بن سودكين النوري له كتاب اسمه "وسائل السائل"، يذكر فيه أجوبة عن مسائل مختلفة تلقاها من الشيخ محي الدين، وربَّما يكون نقلها عنه عندما التقاه بمصر أثناء قدومه من الأندلس، فسأله عن هذه المسائل الموجودة في كتاب "وسائل السائل في الأجوبة عن عيون المسائل"، وكتاب "المعرفة في المسائل الاعتقادية". فيبدو من تحليل الكثير من النصوص والمخطوطات أن هذين الكتابين هما الأصل للعناوين الكثيرة المذكورة أعلاه.[1]

---

[1] هو أبو الطاهر، شمس الدين إسماعيل بن سودكين بن عبد الله النوري: صوفي أصله من تونس، وصحب الشيخ محي الدين، وشرح بعض كتبه، منها التجليات الإلهية. وله كتب أخرى، مثل: لوائح الأسرار ولوائح الأنوار (سبعة أجزاء)، وتحفة التدبير (في الكيمياء)، إضافة إلى كتاب وسائل السائل الذي يبدو أنه جزء مختصر من كتاب لوائح الأسرار ولوائح الانوار. توفي الشيخ ابن

الهيولى)، وهي التي يُكنَّى عنها: بالدرَّة البيضاء، والزمرُّدة الخضراء (والياقوتة الحمراء)، والسُّبحة السوداء، على الترتيب. لذلك كثيراً ما نجد هذه الكتب الثلاثة في مخطوطة واحدة تُسمَّى: "المسائل الثلاث"، وقد نجدها منفردة كذلك.

كما يُلاحظ أنَّ هذه المسائل الثلاث ربَّما تكون هي أيضاً بدورها جزءًا من كتاب آخر يُسمَّى: "الوسائل في الأجوبة عن عيون المسائل"، وهو كتاب موجود بالفعل ويُصنَّف ضمن كتب الشيخ محي الدين، لأنه ذكره في الفهرس وفي الفتوحات المكية، وله مخطوطات كثيرة، ولكنَّها غير مكتملة وبعضها عبارة عن مقاطع مختصرة من بعض أبواب الفتوحات، حيث يبدو كذلك أنَّ الشيخ قد افتتح الفتوحات ببعض هذه المسائل، التي ربَّما يكون قد اختصرها من كتاب الوسائل، ولذلك نجده أيضاً بعناوين أخرى، مثل: "خطبة في نضد العالم"، أو: "خطبة في كيفية ترتيب العالم". وفي مخطوطة يوسف أغا 4868، التي سنذكرها بعد قليل، والتي يبدو أنها مكتوبة بخط الشيخ الأكبر نفسه، يقول في آخرها: "وهذه الخطبة هي خطبة الكتاب الموسوم بالوسائل في الأجوبة عن عيون المسائل".

السبب الذي يدعونا للقول بأن الدرَّة والزمرُّدة والسُّبحة هي "ثلاث مسائل" من ضمن "عيون المسائل" هو أنَّ الشيخ ذكر في آخر السُّبحة ما نصُّه: "وسنذكر طرفاً من بعض الأمور التي وُكِّل بها الأرواح التي لهذه الأفلاك في الجزء الذي فيه

٤

تونس لمدة وجيزة. فربما يكون هذا الكتّاب قد ألَّفه الشيخ في تونس إجابة على سؤال من أحد مريدي صاحبه الشيخ عبد العزيز المهدوي، الذي كان في زيارته هناك للمرة الثانية سنة 598 هـ (وكانت الزيارة الأولى سنة 590 هـ). فنحن نعرف أنه كتب لهم رسالة يحاورهم فيها عن الفرق بين الماهيّة والهويّة، وكذلك بدأ هناك كتابه الشهير: "إنشاء الدوائر والجداول"، ولكنّه لم يستطع أن يكمله في تونس لأنه كان عليه أن يُكمل رحلته نحو مكة المكرّمة بقصد الحج، خاصة وأنه سوف يمرّ بمصر، ليقضي هناك شهر رمضان الكريم مع أصدقاء طفولته أحمد الخياط ومحمد الحريري، ثم يتوجّه إلى مدينة الخليل المباركة، لزيارة أبي الأنبياء سيدنا إبراهيم الخليل، صلَّى الله عليه وسلَّم، ثم يعرج على مدينة المعراج، القدس الشريفة، ومنها يتوجّه إلى المدينة المنوّرة، لزيارة خاتم الأنبياء سيِّدنا محمَّد، صلَّى الله عليه وسلم، قبل بدء شعائر الحج في شهر ذي الحجّة.

كذلك نعلم أنَّ بداية الفتوحات المكية - التي ذكر فيها كتاب العقلة المذكور فيه كتاب الدرة البيضاء - كانت مهداةً إلى صاحبه الشيخ عبد العزيز المهدوي، وفيها ذكر العديد من المسائل الكلامية.

في جميع الأحوال، يعدُّ هذا الكتّاب من الكتب المؤكَّدة نسبتُها إلى الشيخ، رضي الله عنه؛ وهو عبارة عن جواب عن مسألة القلم الأعلى، أو العقل الأوَّل، وهو كثيراً ما يرد ضمن مجموعة من ثلاث مسائل يُفصِّل فيها الشيخ معاني العقل والنفس والجسم (أو

[مقدمة: من قبل محمد حاج يوسف]

هذا نص كتاب "الدرة البيضاء في ذكر مقام القلم الأعلى" للشيخ الأكبر محي الدين ابن العربي، وفق مخطوطة مكتبة ولي الدين، رقم 1821، مع المقارنة ببعض المخطوطات والمطبوعات الأخرى، فقط فيما يخص الكلمات والعبارات التي يمكن أن تغير المعنى.

أما الهوامش والعناوين والإضافات التي بين (قوسين صغيرين)، فهي للشرح وتوضيح بعض الجمل الغامضة، وليست من أصل النص، وكذلك: التشكيل، وعلامات الترقيم، والتقسيم إلى فقرات، وإضافة العناوين [التي بين قوسين متوسطين].

وليس الغرض من هذه الطبعة تحقيق هذا الكتاب، وإصداره باللغة العربية، بل إعداده للترجمة إلى اللغة الإنكليزية ليصدر ضمن كتاب:

(The White Pearl – Names and Descriptions of the Single Monad – Volume III in "Short Treatises by Ibn al-Arabi", Translation and Annotation by Mohamed Haj Yousef)

يعدُّ كتاب الدرة البيضاء من الكتب القديمة، التي ألفها الشيخ الأكبر محي الدين ابن العربي في المرحلة المغربية، أو الأندلسية، فقد صنَّفه قبل سنة 598 هـ، لأنه مذكور في كتاب عقلة المستوفز، المذكور في الأبواب الأولى من الفتوحات المكية، الذي بدأ الشيخ تأليفه في تلك السنة عندما استقرَّ في مكة المكرمة قادماً من الأندلس، بعد أن تنقَّل بين مدن المغرب، وسكن في

Made in the USA
Middletown, DE
29 November 2022